P9-DMI-655

Secrets of Seduction

Brenda Venus

Secrets of Seduction

How to Be the Best Lover Your Woman Ever Had

A DUTTON BOOK

DUTTON

Published by the Penguin Group
Penguin Books USA Inc., 375 Hudson Street,
New York, New York 10014, U.S.A.
Penguin Books Ltd, 27 Wrights Lane, London W8 5TZ, England
Penguin Books Australia Ltd, Ringwood, Victoria, Australia
Penguin Books Canada Ltd, 10 Alcorn Avenue,
Toronto, Ontario, Canada M4V 3B2
Penguin Books (N.Z.) Ltd, 182–190 Wairau Road,
Auckland 10, New Zealand

Penguin Books Ltd, Registered Offices:
Harmondsworth, Middlesex, England

First published by Dutton, an imprint of New American Library,
a division of Penguin Books USA Inc.
Distributed in Canada by McClelland & Stewart Inc.

First Printing, May, 1993
1 2 3 4 5 6 7 8 9 10

Copyright © Brenda Venus, 1993
All rights reserved.

 REGISTERED TRADEMARK—MARCA REGISTRADA

LIBRARY OF CONGRESS CATALOGING-IN-PUBLICATION DATA:
Venus, Brenda.
Secrets of seduction : how to be the best lover your woman ever
had / Brenda Venus.
p.   cm.
ISBN 0-525-93601-7
1. Women—Sexual behavior.   2. Hygiene, Sexual.   I. Title.
HQ29.V46   1993
613.9'6—dc20   92-33513
CIP

Printed in the United States of America
Set in Sabon

Without limiting the rights under copyright reserved above, no
part of this publication may be reproduced, stored in or
introduced into a retrieval system, or transmitted, in any form,
or by any means (electronic, mechanical, photocopying, recording,
or otherwise), without the prior written permission of both the
copyright owner and the above publisher of this book.

To Henry Miller, my mentor. From knowing Henry, I fully understand the importance of his work in pioneering the concept of modern sexuality. Instead of my words, I quote ol' Willie (Shakespeare) to ol' Henry (Miller): "I can no other answer make but thanks and thanks and ever thanks."

I cannot thank you individually, because in writing this book, I tried to touch and was touched by all and every bit of humanity. So I thank you *all*!

Contents

Introduction   1

1—*What Makes a Good Lover*

FEMALE FANTASIES   5   •   CONFIDENCE   7   •
COMMUNICATION   11   •   LAUGHTER MELTS
ICE   18   •   GROOMING   21   •   BODY
LANGUAGE   29   •   SEXUAL CHEMISTRY   32

2—*What Women Want and . . . Don't*

R-E-S-P-E-C-T   37   •   ROMANCE   41   •
ADVENTURES IN LOVE   47   •
TEASING   51   •   WHEN WOMEN
WANT IT   53   •   VIRGINS   56   •
CLASSIC TURN-OFFS   59   •   COLLECTING
STAMPS OR HOW TO GET DUMPED   63

3—*How to Get Started*

WOMEN MEN WANT TO AVOID   69   •   THE
PERFECT WOMAN   74   •   GREAT PLACES TO
MEET WOMEN   78   •   HOW TO KNOW IF A
WOMAN IS INTERESTED   80   •   TIPS FOR THE
FIRST DATE   82   •   TO KISS OR NOT TO
KISS   84   •   HOW TO WINE AND DINE   87

4—*Know Her Body—And Yours*

MALE AND FEMALE SEX ORGANS 99 •
FOREPLAY 106 • CUNNILINGUS 119 •
INTERCOURSE 125 • ORGASM AND THE
G-SPOT 135 • THE VENUS BUTTERFLY AND
OTHER SPECIALTIES 143 • MASTURBATION
FOR MEN 147 • MASTURBATION FOR
WOMEN 151 • THE JOY OF CONDOMS 155

5—*If Things Go Wrong: Troubleshooting*

PREMATURE EJACULATION 163 • WHEN YOU
CAN'T GET IT UP OR KEEP IT UP 167

Epilogue 171

Sex Quiz 173

Bibliography 175

Introduction

*I don't mind living in a man's world as long as I can
be a woman in it.*

—MARILYN MONROE

Would you like to know what 1,500 women throughout the world say pleases them in bed *and* out? That's
about how many women I spoke to while I wrote this
book. And did they talk! Sometimes it took a lot of
wine, laughter, and tears to get them to tell the truth,
but this book is the distillation of the secrets they revealed. If you want to know what women are dying
to tell men but never do, read on.

Every woman is an individual. Each has her own
set of needs and sexual buttons. Still, it's worth knowing a few age-old secrets that *always* work to bring
men and women together.

The first secret I'll let you in on is that a man must
keep a woman stimulated on several levels—mentally,
emotionally, and physically. Sex is not just about
knowing what to do with your hands, mouth, and the
rest of your body; it's about your whole person. Your
day-to-day behavior tells a lot about how you'll be in
bed—at least that's what we women have always
understood.

Don't believe the hype. You don't have to be someone you're not. On the contrary; if you are relaxed
and honest, even *with* any faults, things will start to
happen. Forget all those myths about what women like,
and when and how we like it. Talk to us, ask us, and
try us, instead. It's your *total being* we want—not just

your Eiffel Tower! (And remember: The highest sexual pleasures are experienced when you are fully yourself.)

I wrote this book as a woman who loves and appreciates men. It's my intention to inspire men to be all they can be in life, love, and sex, to develop the highest possibilities of their talents. Good loving can be taught and learned; I intend to help you reach unimagined heights of pleasure, to make out successfully with a woman from your first hello to those incredible days and nights that follow. But you will need tools—tools for a relationship and tools for lovemaking. This book is dedicated to bringing you those skills.

Begin by having a new attitude, one that says: I believe in myself!

You are what you believe. It's time to let go of all regrets. It's time to take charge and to focus your attention on being the man you know you are—the one we can't wait to meet!

1

. . . .

*What
Makes
a Good
Lover*

*To live as gently as I can;
To be, no matter where, a man,
To take what comes of good or ill
And cling to faith and honour still;
To do my best, and let that stand
The record of my brain and hand,
And then, should failure come to
me,
Still work and hope for* victory.
—EDGAR A. GUEST, *My Creed*

FEMALE FANTASIES

Do women like sex for the sake of sex? Yes, yes, and absolutely yes! As you tremble with want for your woman, she too can tremble with lust for her man. Women fantasize about sex as often as men do. Have you ever wanted a girl so much that when you were near her your knees buckled, your hands started to sweat, and your heart skipped a beat? Women have similar feelings.

Some women palpitate from the thought of a certain man. It's like the flutter of tiny butterflies running from the navel down to the inside of the legs. When she walks by, she hopes no one can tell how lost she is in that seductive swoon. Getting into her car, she fantasizes about how exciting you would be in the throes of passion. She thinks about you all the way home. Then she recreates those thoughts over and over again in the secrecy of her bedroom. It's possible not one word was ever spoken, just an exchanged glance —a look!

You're at the grocery store, she might be standing behind you. She might be handing you papers at work. She might be flirting with you at a party. Her subconscious feelers are always out on a quest for her knight in shining armor. You seldom realize that you are the hero of a lady's fantasy—a lady with a fertile and vivid imagination!

Just as you get turned on by watching a woman, a woman derives tremendous pleasure from watching you. The way you move, open a door, walk across the room, read a book, play sports, work out, or even pick up a glass of water. She's checking out your body rhythm and character.

Watching is titillating, especially when the one you're watching is graceful and lovely. Maybe you like to watch your girlfriend or wife walk around in high heels and a teddy. Well, a woman has fantasies, too. Some like to think of you in jeans and no shirt, others like underwear and an unbuttoned shirt or a soft silk robe with your naked body underneath. You may be stunned to know that some women imagine you masturbating—a big turn-on for lots of ladies. Whatever your woman's fancy may be, do it for her from time to time. It keeps the passion alive.

Heidi, a beautiful and provocative friend of mine, said, "When I cook dinner for my boyfriend, I turn up the heat so he'll feel uncomfortable and disrobe. He's painfully shy, so I have to encourage him to remove his shirt. I love looking at his chest and his beautiful arms. After dinner, I pull his jeans off, ask him to change the music, and pour the wine—anything I can think of just to watch him move!"

We dream and dream. What if you surprised her? Maybe, after you've seen a seductive movie together, you drop a hint, like, "Didn't you just love that bathtub scene with all those candles filling the room? I could almost smell them and feel the heat coming off the screen." You tell her it sure looked exciting, with a twinkle in your eye.

Don't be surprised if she replies, "I loved the scene in *Body Heat* when he makes love to her for the first time on the floor." Maybe she wants you to take charge (many women do), so rent the movie and study the scene. (Note that William Hurt was passionate, sexual and sensual, but *not* rough.)

If you want to know what our fantasies are like,

think about the scene in *No Way Out* in which Kevin Costner makes love to Sean Young in the back seat of a moving limousine, or when he paints Susan Sarandon's toenails while she is tied to the bed by her wrists in *Bull Durham*; or consider Dennis Quaid in *The Big Easy* when he uses his hand to bring Ellen Barkin to orgasm. Make sure you check out the hair-raising scenes between Mickey Rourke and Kim Basinger in *9½ Weeks*. And, ohh . . . *Basic Instinct*—the way Michael Douglas made love to both gorgeous women. *That was hot!* Catch Willem Dafoe in *Body of Evidence* with the Blonde Bomb rock star.

Not all our fantasies are so elaborate. We also dream of a glass of our favorite wine and a massage. It's not long before our minds wander, though, back to you, in bed.

One of the most common female fantasies is being loosely tied up, with their man's hands, lips, and tongue making love to their entire bodies. Keep reading and I'll tell you how to make fantasies even better than this one come true!

See how we've gone from a woman's first fantasy about you, directly to you and the lucky lady, wild in bed together? It's really not so farfetched. And that's why I'm here: To tell you *exactly* how to get from that first glance to the most intimate and steamy sexual ecstasy imaginable.

CONFIDENCE

Once I went to an art opening for my friend Zachary. Not knowing a soul there except the artist, I glanced across the gallery, where about four hundred people mingled. The first person to catch my eye was a man at the other end of the room who positively *reeked* of confidence. Oozing from his every pore was the attitude

Look at *me, I'm somebody*. The man was Steven Segal—*before* he had made his first film. Now, *that's* star quality!

Women love men who have confidence. Nothing's more sexually exciting than a man with a feeling of certainty about himself; a man who knows how to move, how to dress, how and when to touch a woman. I'm not talking about "macho" or "cocky"—that's *pretending* to be a man. I mean the kind of man whose assuredness springs from the depths of his soul. He's genuinely positive; he doesn't pose or assume a phony attitude. He's as real as a tiger!

This kind of man attracts women without even trying. Women will want him because he's energetic, dynamic, charismatic and they can tell there is more to his life than just women. He's a man who will love passionately, but will never smother. He's able to treat others with respect because he respects himself. He has the courage to turn defeat into victory, and yet he remains vulnerable.

This guy will deliver. He's able to make his woman feel secure and protected. He's not in a hurry. He takes his time to get to know a woman.

A man who doesn't mince words or waste time savors every moment he's with her. He's direct and straightforward with diplomacy. A woman wants that "male" thing, meaning she wants to feel his strengths—physically as her protector, emotionally as her confidant and friend, and mentally as her equal. She also wants to be pursued by someone she adores. Perhaps you hesitate because you fear her or you fear commitment. If you like her, stake your claim and mine it—who knows what gold you might discover. Any woman prefers a man who knows what he wants and goes after it.

Best of all, a confident man truly listens to a woman. "Most men hear, but don't listen," says Tess, a professor at Vassar. The confident man listens to every word his love utters and uses his own barometer to evaluate her, but he won't try to manipulate her mind. That's listening!

Building confidence with the woman you want can be tough initially. All first steps are difficult, and everyone experiences self-doubt, disappointment, and frustration sometimes. When you were a child and you took your first steps it wasn't easy. Breaking the ice with a ravishing woman is not easy—but nothing worthwhile is.

Here's a little secret about women. We feel insecure when we're enamored with a man. Our lips mumble as if they were rubber, our eyes get stuck in their sockets, our voices sound as if an alien being has invaded our bodies. We constantly wring our hands, blush, and say the dumbest things. Sound familiar? It happens to *everyone*.

Just to let you know that feeling anxious is a perfectly normal response to pressure and stress, consider that twenty-six million Americans will suffer from anxiety of one sort or another during their lifetime. It's ahead of depression and drug abuse.

Why, the first time I was interviewed by Clint Eastwood for a role in his film, *The Eiger Sanction*, I was scared to death. His rugged good looks, laid-back demeanor, and self-confidence left me stunned. Adrenaline was rushing through my veins, and I felt like I acted foolishly during the entire meeting. As if that experience weren't enough, walking back to my car, burning with frustration, I kicked a car tire and a heel on one of my new high-heel shoes snapped off. What next, I thought, while removing the other shoe and throwing it over a fence. Feeling ridiculous and stupid, I happened to look up and see Clint standing in a window with a Cheshire grin. He had witnessed my entire tantrum! I nodded my head and burst out laughing. Miraculously, he did too! (I got the part.)

What I felt was comparable to stage fright with its rush of adrenaline. Even the great actor Sir Laurence Olivier said he couldn't give a dynamic performance without it. Use nerves to your advantage: Let them excite you, then ignite you. Consider it a challenge and rise to the occasion.

Confidence means not dwelling on your imperfections. Everybody's got them. Who knows—maybe she'll think your shortcomings are charming and fall in love with you because of them. Don't laugh! Isn't it true that it's that slight "flaw" in a woman—that beauty mark she always hated, legs she always thought were too long and skinny, or an ear she finds a little droopy—that you find irresistible? Remember, a man who truly likes himself puts a woman at ease.

Enthusiasm and a *positive attitude* are terrific turn-ons. When a man shows up at my door, I want to see a twinkle in his eye telling me he's just thrilled to be there and he's ready to have fun. A man should exude a healthy lust for life, so his woman knows that she's in for a great time.

TROUBLESHOOTING

If you feel negative feelings taking over, *stop*. Reassure yourself by remembering past successes and triumphs. Remember the things you really like about yourself, and feel grateful and blessed because of them. Maybe you're a computer wiz, or you've got a perfect nose, or you sing, or play the piano or guitar. Maybe you do magic tricks with your "family jewels." Everyone's got something special . . . dwell on *that!*

And remember the wisdom of Ralph Waldo Emerson: "Enthusiasm is one of the most powerful engines of success. When you do a thing, do it with all your might. Put your whole soul into it. . . . Nothing great was ever achieved without enthusiasm."

Don't speak negatively; people who do are down-ers, boring, and a big zero on the fun meter. Don't put down the woman you're with—or anyone else for that matter, including yourself. You might think it's amus-ing, but it's not. Look for the best in every person and situation. But please don't dwell excessively on the at-tributes of other men—your lady will wonder why she's not with any of them!

Developing confidence takes time, patience, and a willingness to let go of your insecurities. But it's worth the effort. Confidence gets you one step closer to the delights awaiting you in the rest of this book. And believe me—you don't want to miss them for the world!

COMMUNICATION

The first ingredient in conversation is truth; next, good sense; the third, good humor; and the fourth, wit.
—SIR WILLIAM TEMPLE

It goes without saying that you can't ask a woman for a date without talking to her first. Communication, however, doesn't always mean talking; once you're in bed, body language takes over. But long before you get physical, you communicate to a woman with your total being, both tangible and intangible—eyes, face, body, presence, and attitude. Good communication—from day one—leads to good lovemaking for both partners.

HONESTY

The first rule is to be honest. This is a must! Don't open your mouth unless you say something you believe to be true. I love clarity in a man and clarity can only come from the truth. A real man knows the one guiding principle that governs the universe is: what goes around, comes around. That's why his compass points to true north. So say *exactly* what you mean, and mean *exactly* what you say—even in the heat of passion. And when you speak, project your voice from down low, at the diaphragm—it sounds more sincere. And a full voice is sensual and sexy.

If a woman feels you're being honest, she'll let down her barriers. The more we women believe in you and trust you, the more we start to relax and smile. Only then can we truly enjoy who you are as a man and allow your romantic advances to begin working on our female sensibilities.

LISTENING

The second golden rule is to listen. It's simple: If you're interested, you become *interesting*. A woman equates good listeners with good lovers. If you listen to her in life, she intuitively believes you will listen to her silent signals in bed. If you don't listen, you won't hear her music, so how do you expect to play a successful duet?

A woman can spot a bad lover a mile away: He's the guy across the table who's talking about himself all night, not listening to anyone. I don't care if you're Abraham Lincoln, monologues are terribly unattractive. Even if your subject is genuinely interesting to the woman you're with, to go on and on, hogging the conversation, is selfish and repulsive. Whether it's Dostoyevsky or the Retail Price Index you're expounding upon, it's overkill and self-defeating.

Looking and listening for a woman's inner truth without imposing your own fear, envy, comparison, and judgment will enable you to hear what she is *really* saying. Don't let your previous history bias your receptivity to a new experience. Listen to your lady's point of view. Instead of trying to change it or convince her otherwise, show some interest in *her* opinion. Be glad she has one! If you take the emphasis off yourself and put it on her, you'll be amazed at her reaction.

Let's put listening and self-confidence into action. Here's how it could work: First, you'll need to get into a receptive mood—ready to smoothly approach a woman, introduce yourself, and learn about her, because the old, used-car sales pitch won't work. Think confident, think focus, think calm. Find a way to relax—run around the block, masturbate. It doesn't matter what you do, the bottom line is *calm down*. Then go to the party.

OK, you're at the party. Notice that attractive woman across the room? You're definitely calm, right? Make eye contact with her a few times. Don't forget: It's a slow rhythm you need. Fast movements could scare her away.

If you think she likes the way your trousers hang, approach her. But don't try to knock her unconscious with the first few words out of your mouth. A straightforward, simple introduction is a successful opening line: "Hi, my name's John." Extend your hand; if you've read her silent signals correctly she'll offer you her hand and tell you her name. (By the way, avoid calling her "honey," "babe," "sweetie," or other insulting nicknames. We like hearing our own names, not your abbreviations and assumptions. To women, hearing their names in conversation is a compliment.)

If she's responding favorably and smiling, ask her about her weekend or her week. With sensitivity and style, probe a little into her background. Where is she from? What college did she go to? What books has she read? What are her artistic interests? Is she musically inclined? Does she like sports? What movies has she seen lately? Who are her favorite writers? Poets? Movie stars? Does she like her job? What did she do today?

Ask questions that you'd sincerely like answers to. People love to talk about themselves. In fact, she will probably appreciate your curiosity and reciprocate by asking you questions. Both of you will relax and you'll know when the time is right to tell her about things that mean something to *you*—things that touch, move, and excite you. Then the ball's rolling.

As you chat at the party, listen carefully to what she says. Don't just let her words fall like rain—catch them and taste their essence. If you can't agree with her, at least try to empathize and relate. Don't pity— that's not constructive—but do share her feelings. If she begins to discuss a certain problem, changing the subject to football isn't a wise move. Maybe she would like your opinion.

As she speaks, observe her gestures. Look for things to compliment—her hair, hands, jewelry, clothes, perfume, complexion, eyes, nose, the way she walks, her voice, her laugh—whatever pleases you about her. Find things that usually go unnoticed, like her ears, dimples, the cleft in her chin, a beauty mark on her cheek, the unusual color of her eyes or arch of her eyebrows. When giving compliments, always be truthful. A woman instinctively knows when you're being dishonest, and she'll put you instantly in her "loser" slot.

I strongly believe you should stay away from sexual comments early on. Some women are extremely shy, or they take great offense to your first noticing anything physical. If you're patient, you'll have plenty of time later to let her know how much you're turned on by her physical attributes. If it feels absolutely right and you have no doubts, maybe the third date. But don't get too personal too soon. Women today like to take a little longer to get to know you for all the obvious reasons.

The bottom line is, be yourself and be honest. Take stock of whom you're talking to before you speak. Never recite other people's opinions—a human parrot is a real turn-off. Share your knowledge, experiences, and deeply held beliefs with her, and she'll do the same.

EMOTIONS—YOURS!

For most men, being honest, communicative, and sensitive is difficult. From an early age they are taught that "boys don't cry." A boy learns that feelings are considered feminine, and if he expresses his feelings he will seem girlish. Not so! At least not today.

A woman wants a man who thinks with his heart, not just his intellect or his "Empire State Building." She wants him to express himself. One of the last great American originals, Henry Miller, dedicated his life to fighting for self-expression. In the 1960s, he became a role model, a father of that decade and decades to come because his fight allowed you to do the same—express yourself!

You would be surprised just how much a woman will bend to a sensitive, gentle man who is not afraid to express himself. I know being vulnerable takes courage, but if you lose courage, you lose everything a man stands for. Consider the scene in *Gone With the Wind* when Clark Gable, playing the dashing Rhett Butler, breaks down and cries in front of Melanie. The director had to argue for days to get Gable to do that scene; the star thought he would be laughed at, and his career would be affected. With much ado, they finally convinced Gable that it was actually the only way to play the scene.

When the film opened, Gable became a national hero and won again the hearts of millions of women. Men in all walks of life began to imitate him because women had fallen in love with a new kind of hero. Gable's character had courage, strength, and vulnerability. The "mothering instinct" may explain why women want to take strong, vulnerable men to their breast. That's a cozy place to be for showing a little courage, don't you think?

A woman will offer all the help you need to share your feelings. She will spend countless hours enchanting a man into forgetting his inhibitions. She'll wear sexy clothes, painted nails, a new hairdo, exotic perfume . . . anything to transport him from his "real world" of work, sports, and hobbies into her magic realm of feelings. Other women find wearing sexy clothes, etc., a bit troubling and unnatural. They prefer making a man feel completely at ease, rather than aroused, actually accomplishing the same goal in a more comfortable and genuine atmosphere.

One block to better communication is the fact that men are more likely to use the left side of the brain, the side associated with facts, calculations, and logic, while women tend to use the right side of their brains, for guidance. It's been called "women's intuition"— an inner wisdom that cannot be scientifically proven or explained. The ideal, of course, would be a balanced combination of both hemispheres. Women could try to better understand some of a man's logic, and men could make a special effort to loosen up and give a little freedom to their instincts.

Until there's some magic solution for balancing your left and right brain, you'll wonder, "How do I go about getting in touch with my feelings without going into therapy?" Involve yourself in group activities. It could be an acting class, it could be a twelve-step group like Alcoholics Anonymous or CODA. By the way, you don't have to be an alcoholic or drug abuser to attend these meetings. The message is universal and can help you with other problems. Any place where feelings are freely expressed will be liberating. Also, try talking to a trusted friend. Or drive to the top of a mountain and scream yourself into exhaustion—a therapy Richard Burton often used. He did it not only to lower his voice but to free himself of anxiety. Getting your feelings out in the open is easier than it may seem, and it works wonders.

Not that baring your emotions will come into play on the first date. More likely, you'll need this later as you become closer. But the one lesson for early meetings is don't be a stoic; put some honest feeling into your "rap." *That's* communication!

One final thought: By expressing yourself, I don't mean saying to a woman you admire, "Gee, those lips! You look like you could suck a golf ball through a garden hose!" This kind of charm will get a kick where you don't want it instead of a stroke where you do. At times like this, think what a poet like Pablo Neruda, or your own special hero, would say. "Mmmm, I sure envy your lipstick!"

Learn from the great masters, like David Fisher, who wrote the famous line, "If I told you you have a beautiful body, would you hold it against me?" There's always a way to express yourself in a sexy manner without being crude. Crudeness is usually a sign of insecurity. Honesty, sincerity, and politeness will get you everywhere.

TROUBLESHOOTING

"What if it doesn't work?" you ask. If anything *can* work, it's good, honest, lively communication. But sometimes things don't click. No one said the road to seduction is a short one.

Have faith in yourself. Make sure that you get what you want by asking yourself three things: What do I want? What is standing in the way of what I want? What is the most direct action to take to get what I want? And, don't let "no" get you down— pause, reevaluate, and bounce back. Make sure you know exactly what you want *before* you go after it. And be careful what you wish for . . . you just may get it!

Don't ever give up on yourself and be quick at seizing advantages. If you discover she didn't like your flowers, try chocolate the next time. If chocolate doesn't work, try champagne, if champagne doesn't work, try standing on your head. If you keep putting it out, sooner or later she's bound to take the bait.

Persistence often does win the prize, both in life and in love. There have been a number of men in my life whom I rejected at first who, *because of their persistence*, I ended up sharing parts of my life with. Jeff, for example, a professional baseball player, pursued me for almost a year. For many reasons, I was adamant about not getting involved with a professional athlete. Nothing could change my mind, or so I thought! Jeff kept it up: phone calls, charming letters, cards, flowers, candies, thoughtful little presents, tickets to his games, etc. I acquiesced for a lunch. Over a bottle of Taittinger Rosé, delicious pasta, veal picatta, a green salad, zabaglione, and espresso, I fell in love with his humor, intelligence, and lust for life. We ended up spending several years together. A man who knows what he wants and goes after it, deserves my admiration.

Have courage! Heighten your sensibilities! Reveal yourself! Take risks! Use all of your abilities and better qualities to create not just a bridge between you and your partner, but an unbreakable bond.

LAUGHTER MELTS ICE

Humor is what you haven't got when you ought to have it.

—LANGSTON HUGHES

How true it is! I find people are too afraid to look ridiculous, too afraid of what other people may think, too afraid of stepping in cow manure. Well, forget that! Everybody steps in it at one time or another.

How you look when you're standing in it is all that matters! After all, you're the one who has to look in the mirror every day, and to be able to laugh at yourself will get you through the night. Humor is your greatest asset.

My friend Mario has a huge nose, tiny hands, big feet, and stands five feet five inches tall—not to mention the little tufts of hair on his large head. For their first date together, Mario took a very attractive, tall blonde named Sarah to see the classic 1920s movie, *Valentino*, because she said in one of their phone conversations she was interested in the romantic star. In keeping with the tone of the evening, they dined at an Italian restaurant.

After dinner Mario presented Sarah with a picture book about Valentino. He asked her if she would honor him with a few more minutes of her charming company and join him at his house for a little surprise. She was filled with anticipation as they approached his cottage. Once in the house, he lit candles and incense, poured Sarah a glass of red wine, and disappeared into the bedroom. . . .

When he returned, he was wearing a Valentino suit, black slicked-back wig, and a Valentino face mask. In the seductive manner of her 1920s idol, he turned on exotic music, gracefully lit a cigarette, and gazed at her with deep, smoldering glances, à la Valentino. He made her laugh with his antics—and held his hand out for her to dance a tango with him. They moved rhythmically across the floor. But Mario was a bit too creative with his dance, and in his effort to scoop Sarah into his arms, he dropped her on the floor!

As he leaned down to pick her up, this normally shy girl was laughing so hard that she lost her inhibitions and passionately kissed Mario all over his masked face. She ripped off his mask and let loose with a deep, wet delicious kiss that lasted all night long.

Mario wasn't expecting anything, and look at the prize he landed!

Not every man can play like Mario, nor should he. Mario is an actor and is simply doing what he does best, just as you must. But notice what a monumental effort he makes in trying to please a woman, and that eventually, it works and he wins. He's not afraid to make fun of himself, and he's good at finding humor in almost every situation. He's positive, he knows his good qualities, uses them to his advantage, and gives all of himself at every moment. No woman could ask for more.

A hearty laugh opens the door to a woman's heart. A good lover doesn't take himself too seriously. So show enthusiasm! Have a twinkle in your eye when you look at her. For above all else—looks, success, wealth, and power—a woman is attracted to a man with a sense of humor.

History is full of famous men who perfected the talent for charming women and making them laugh despite physical imperfections, a lack of success, or a lack of other qualities. Humor was their allure, wit was their power. The mind is the lover's great ally and equalizer in the eyes of women. Cyrano de Bergerac—endowed with a nose as large as Pinnocchio's—falls in love with the beautiful Roxanne, but never in his wildest dreams does he expect her to return his love.

As the story goes, the humorous and poetic Cyrano writes love letters to Roxanne for a handsome young soldier who can't write a word, much less a sonnet. Roxanne falls in love with the beautiful soldier because of the poems. At the end of the story, when the truth surfaces, Roxanne realizes that Cyrano was the man behind the words and, holding him in her arms as he dies, she professes that it was he, Cyrano, she loved all along. True brilliance, personality, and wit will prevail. And laughter is an aphrodisiac. If a man has the power to make a woman laugh from her gut or deep in her soul, she will adore him and give a lot of herself in return, if not *everything*.

To test the waters of a woman's sense of humor, you can begin with a few inoffensive jokes and double entendres. If the woman responds favorably and understands your humor, you can become more adventurous. If she has a quizzical look on her face and you feel like all your jokes are going nowhere, move on.

You should never be afraid to express your sense of humor, but do have some regard for the other person listening. If you're the only one laughing after each joke, let that be a clue. You don't have to be a rocket scientist to know when you're not being well received. Being on the same wave length with a woman is crucial. So *pay attention!*

Whether you're a man with a natural talent for humor, a sense of timing, or a cool, dry wit, or you're trying to learn these skills, it makes no difference—*go for it!* It's all about making a woman comfortable enough to relax in your presence; *laughter can melt ice*. The more you make her laugh, the more open she becomes and you're halfway home. So be that bodacious hunk of a man who feels good . . . making her feel *great!* And try not to look startled when she begins to kiss you all over!

GROOMING

Costly thy habit as thy purse can buy, But not express'd in fancy; rich, not gaudy; For the apparel oft proclaims the man.

—SHAKESPEARE, Hamlet

Good grooming is about making the most out of what you've got. Do you know that women honestly feel more comfortable with an average guy who presents himself well than with a super-looking guy who intimidates them? So don't worry if you couldn't make the cover of *Gentleman's Quarterly*; it's not important.

It's wrong to confuse pride in your appearance with vanity. A vain man is insecure—always looking in the mirror. And when he looks into a woman's eyes, he's not looking at her, he's trying to catch himself in their reflection. His conversation is laced with impressive names and intellectual narratives, trying desperately to convince everyone (especially himself!) of his self-worth. He's famous for: "Gee, I've been talking about myself all night. Let's talk about you for a minute. Tell me, how do *you* feel about me?"

Mae Beth, a thirty-four-year-old secretary in Washington, D.C., says, "If a guy is too calculated about his looks, it makes me feel unsettled—like he would take better care of his clothes than he would me!"

CHOOSING YOUR THREADS

Be your own man, create your own style. Wear things you've obviously chosen and thought about. You won't attract many women if you are careless about how you look, because they'll think you're careless about how you live—and careless about how you will treat them. So men, tuck in your shirt and stomach, put your shoulders back, hold your head high, and be creative and original. Think well of yourself and she'll think well of you!

All the well-dressed men I know look "at home" in their clothes. They wear their clothes rather than have their clothes wear them. Or if one day you see everybody wearing their clothes backward and you feel stupid, don't do it. If you feel uncomfortable in an Armani suit, don't wear it! No one should force you to wear something you don't like; whose body is it, anyway??

When in doubt about your wardrobe, it's better to underdress than overdress. Simple, elegant, and chic is the key. If you have a problem in the image department, ask a close woman friend for assistance. Women *love* to help a man in this situation.

With a clean body, clean clothes, your own style, and a relaxed posture, you'll look and feel like a million-dollar man, a man with an irresistible glow and women will find themselves instinctively attracted to you. I've seen this happen many times. Remember, you never get a second chance to make a first impression —and we're quick, guys, very, very quick!

EXERCISE

Men, would you like to know what turns on most of the 1,500 women I talked to? It's definitely not the labels on your clothing, but rather what's underneath them. They could not emphasize enough the importance of being physically healthy. A well-tuned, healthy body is an infallible turn-on for a woman.

Do you want to increase your sex appeal? Then you must exercise regularly. By doing this, you will increase your level of testosterone, the mighty male hormone that controls your sex drive. And with greater physical activity, the blood is able to circulate more efficiently through your genitalia, making it easier for your muscles to store glycogen, their needed fuel. Ergo, your sex drive is heightened and your mighty male member is more equipped to perform feats of endurance and stamina!

Have you ever watched Arnold Schwarzenegger or Lee Haney work out in a movie or on television? The sweat pouring off their bodies, the grunts, the moans, the heavy breathing, the release, the *satisfac-*

tion—nothing else in the world can create those feelings, except maybe great sex! Now I'm not telling you to run down to Gold's Gym and become a gladiator or power lifter. I'm simply saying that women love a well-toned body and it's *muy grande* on the list of turnons. So get into the habit of exercising. Not only will you feel better, look better, and have more confidence, but when you take your clothes off, you'll be proud to have her look at your beautiful, naked body.

MR. CLEAN GETS WHAT HE WANTS

All of the women I interviewed agree on one point: One of the single most important factors that attracts them to a man is cleanliness. Knowing that you look and smell good is a turn-on both for you and for her. You need to appeal to all of her senses—touch, taste, smell, sight, and sound. My friend Paul said, "When I take a long time in a hot shower to scrub every part of my body, then put on my favorite clothes and aftershave, there's not a man alive who can touch me. I know I'm clean!"

A great scent can easily evoke eroticism in a woman. For instance, my plane had just arrived in New Orleans when my cousin Rachel came to fetch me and quickly swooped me off to Antoine's for lunch. We were escorted to a table that was set up for three. With an arched eyebrow, I look quizzically at Rachel and asked, "So . . . who are we expecting?" Rachel replied, "There's someone I'd like you to meet. I've been talking you up a bit, hope you don't mind. My sixth sense tells me he's just your type."

A short while passed and it looked as though he wasn't coming, so we ordered our salads. Rachel suddenly looked up and said, "Frank, I'm glad you could make it!" He apologized for the delay, but he was tied up in litigation. I had been tired, when all of a sudden I found myself full of energy. Inhaling deeply as Frank sat down, I smelled something that was intoxicating. Rachel was right . . . he was divine!

I sat silently watching him talk, and move his hands, and every so often I would lean a bit closer to breathe in his cologne. My, my, that was some scent! He was wearing Giorgio's V.I.P. Special Reserve. Amazing what a special kind of man wearing a divine scent can do to a woman's sensibilities!

Most women prefer a man who wears a subtle, fresh, clean, elegant fragrance—it stirs their desire in such an irresistible way! Some time-proven winners would include such scents as Frank's, Hugo Boss, Annick Goutal's Vétiver, Guerlain's Habit Rouge, Givenchy's Gentleman, Hermes' Equipage, Montana's Homme, Bijan, Dior's Eau Savage, Giorgio Armani, Halston's Z-14, Aramis' Eau de Cologne, Victor's Acqua di Selva. Certain mountain men types smell good in Caswell Massey's Patchouly, Sandalwood, and other oils. Always treat yourself to the best; it shows you're a quality man! And if you're strapped for money, then just save it for a special purchase; a bottle of cologne lasts a long time.

There are a few women who do not enjoy cologne on their men; some prefer a natural masculine scent. That's fine; you need to be sensitive to your woman's wants and tastes. But *all* women like a clean, good-smelling man with washed hair and short, buffed nails. Manicured fingernails and toenails are best, but without polish. And if you do use cologne, it should be used to entice, not bulldoze.

KISS OF DEATH

Bad breath is lonely breath, and it can be the *kiss of death*. I couldn't even think of kissing a man with foul breath. It's such a turn-off, and can make some women gag. (Be sure to stay away from garlic or onions when you're trying to woo a woman—unless, of course, she is sharing the garlic with you!)

If you're a highly strung person with a nervous stomach, take care to drink milk or some antacid before you go out on a date, because an upset stomach can cause bad breath. Brush and floss your teeth regularly—and brush your tongue. Have on hand at all times mints, spray, or gum to freshen your mouth, especially if you smoke. There is nothing worse for a nonsmoker than to kiss a smoker. And remember to always ask your date if she minds before you light up. It's courteous.

BODY MOVEMENT

You may not be Cary Grant or Fred Astaire, I know, but that doesn't mean you can't learn from their example. Everybody has to learn from somebody, so why not pick the best in a particular field? Watch the way Kevin Costner moves his body in any one of his films. You could learn a lot by studying his loose style.

Body movement is a universally sensual and pleasurable experience. It's indicative of how sexual a person is. Dancing is sexual body movement in its purest form. It's a great way to meet a woman, but the more you get into body movement in general, the more women will watch your moves. Start by taking dance lessons—Cary Grant did.

If dancing is not for you, then try martial arts, gymnastics, or any class that can teach you to move your body gracefully. I assure you, not only will it come in handy in everyday life, it will also boost your confidence in the bedroom. Changing sexual positions requires rhythm, timing, and *grace*. (There's nothing worse than an accidental elbow in the face or a knee in the groin.)

HAIR

Beards and moustaches look great on certain men. They can camouflage facial weaknesses, such as a pointed or smallish chin, while drawing attention to your better features. If you have a thin upper lip, but your bottom lip is nice and full, a moustache would be flattering. If your facial hair is coarse, try using a conditioner. Let it grow a bit longer and comb the moustache hair over the lip instead of straight down like a dagger. But in the event your lady recoils instead of purrs when you lean over to kiss her, it's time to consider a shave. Ask the lady in question how she feels about it.

A good smelling, clean, healthy head of hair is enticing to a lot of women. Just as you men find a woman's hair sexy, we women find a man's hair sexy. I, particularly, like to cut, shampoo, and condition my man's hair.

The key to a healthy head of hair is daily washing and scalp massage with a good shampoo and conditioner, plenty of fresh air, a balanced diet, sunshine, and stress eliminators, such as exercising, sports, playing a musical instrument, gardening, walking outdoors, visiting an amusement park or museum, shopping, or watching a comedy show. Napoleon Bonaparte relieved his stress with daily hot baths. The more stress, the hotter the water, the longer the bath.

Carpentry as a hobby can be relaxing. Harrison Ford was a carpenter before he became a movie star. He said it makes him feel good to build when he's not making films. Do whatever pleases you. You don't need permission—just do it! I guarantee it will help you keep your hair for more years even if you're fighting genetics.

Let's say you've tried everything, and you still find excessive amounts of hair in your brush every morning. Now is the time to ask your dermatologist about hair plugs or Rogaine. Rogaine is more efficacious when you have thinning hair, rather than none at all. So if you care, act now . . . before it's too late!

If you've got a well-receded hairline and have a well-shaped head, you might consider shaving the rest off, like Yul Brynner or Michael Jordan. It's so sexy to see and feel a beautiful bald head. One of the women I interviewed, Monique, a Parisian model, said her boyfriend uses Nair with aloe vera for the best results. I've seen many good-looking men with receding hairlines that I find very sexy, indeed. Whatever makes you feel the most comfortable and the most attractive, go for it!

Now let's address the man with a less than perfectly shaped head, who is losing hair at great speed. In the event you've tried all possibilities and nothing has worked for you, it's time to check out a toupee. Many a handsome man has worn a toupee and no one ever knew. Toupees can look completely natural.

BODY HAIR

I have a lot to say about body hair! Women like hair. "The more hair, the more like her Teddy Bear." Some women enjoy playing with your chest hair. They bury their faces in it, roll their fingers around it and even lick it. However, unkempt or excessive hair in other places might make you feel uncomfortable about your appearance. If so, there are several ideas you could try, depending on your likes and dislikes. Hair on your back or any place it displeases you can be easily eliminated with regular waxing or electrolysis. The results are praiseworthy, but treatment can be expensive. If you'd rather not remove it, cocoa butter and unscented lotions not only soften the body hair, they also make the skin smooth to a woman's touch and there's nothing better than having skin she wants to kiss and touch all over. Right? There are women who prefer smooth-chested men. That particular look has a beauty of its own. Body builders shave their entire bodies before a contest to enhance their muscular definition.

For your pubic hairs, I would recommend conditioning and trimming. Just as you might trim your fingernails, toenails, and unwanted calluses once a week or every few weeks, you should also trim the hairs in your nose (use special scissors, don't pluck. It could cause infection), on your toes, in your ears, and possibly the ones under your arms. It's simple maintenance. I've talked to a few women who actually find it erotic to lather, shave, and trim their boyfriends' bodies. They said it gives them a feeling of power. Hmmm . . .

SKIN

A sauna or steam bath is very healthy for the body and skin. Native Americans used sweat lodges before going into battle, believing it rid the body of impurities and evil spirits, which enabled them to fight better. Every person should sweat daily for healthy skin and a clear mind.

Skin care is just as important for men as it is for women. For your face, you need to use a moisturizer, especially under the eyes. Cleanse your skin well every day and treat yourself to a facial from time to time. You deserve it! Warren Beatty and George Hamilton would certainly agree. They do a lot to maintain their handsome faces. Take another look at Warren's facial care in the movie *Bugsy*. Why not do the same for yourself?

BODY LANGUAGE

Of all flirtatious gestures, 84 percent are initiated by women. Amazed? Then maybe you're part of the percentage of men who are totally unaware of them. If you're not paying attention to the body language of women, you're missing out on some fantastic opportunities.

Studies show that 66 percent of all communication is nonverbal, so pay close attention to the way a woman moves, what she does with her hands, her legs, her posture, and especially her eyes. If she gives you that longer-than-necessary look—when her eyes lock with yours for a long moment, then turn away—that's your signal to proceed.

Eye contact is far more effective than touching a woman after first meeting her. (Some women can practically orgasm looking in the right man's eyes.) Giving her time and space to trust you is more important and rewarding than diving in without assessing the situation. When the time is right, she'll let you know by her body language.

When a woman does feel comfortable enough, you'll know. Watch for these signs: stroking her hair seductively, thrusting her breasts forward, rolling her hips as she walks away, winking, wetting her lips, caressing her face or another part of her body (or yours!), fondling her glass in surrogate fashion, crossing her legs in your direction, brushing her thigh against yours, or adjusting your shirt collar or hair. These are a few ways that a woman will tell you she is interested.

If you're not sure, watch her a little longer and more carefully to pick up any sexual signals she might be giving off unwittingly—or deliberately—for your eyes only. You don't want to miss these! (Reflections in shiny objects and mirrors or quick glances are not intrusive—staring is!)

When I like a man, a light goes on inside. My eyes sparkle, and my look usually translates as, "Honey, what you don't have, you'll never need!" I grin like a cat who's swallowed a canary, and my hands are usually fidgety—touching either my hair, face, corners of my clothing, earrings, or other such things. I sit and stand tall and my walk has more of a swing. I become intensely interested in every word he utters, every move he makes. And no other man in the world exists but him. In other words, my whole being changes as I start to see Mr. Right!

When women initiate flirting gestures they are not saying, "I want to sleep with you," but rather, "I find you interesting and I would like to get to know you better." Inexperienced men often try to come on too quickly to the most beautiful woman in a room, and more often than not, they fail. An experienced man will wait patiently for glances of interest before he makes a move. His secret motto is, "I can wait, and I can do without. But not for too long!"

TROUBLESHOOTING: WARMING THE COLD SHOULDER
An experienced man knows that a negative body signal does not necessarily mean "Stop." It simply means "Proceed with caution." The woman may like you, but she could be feeling scared, nervous, or shy. The reason she's tense isn't important. What is important is that you demonstrate the exact opposite of her tight, tense attitude. When you talk to her, make sure you're open, relaxed, and smiling with confidence. A little humor could break the final barrier. Give her a lot of physical personal space and keep your posture fluid and easy, with your arms open. She will begin to mirror your positive movements and you will form a connection. This kind of understated persistence is a compliment to a woman.

Some negative body signals are crossing her arms, locking her ankles, putting her arms around her knees, holding her handbag tight in her lap, acting distracted in conversation, looking all around the room, having a superior attitude, looking bored, yawning, picking lint off her clothes, or looking at her watch.

When a woman displays negative body language, first ask yourself what is the overall impression she's giving. If her eyes are telling you to come hither, but her body is in a locked position, then I would say that you have a good chance of relaxing her and opening her up with your positive and confident attitude.

If neither her eyes nor her body language inspire confidence, don't worry. Sometimes, it's just not meant to be. When you see the following signals for an extended period of time, it's time to hang it up: a slight, rather aloof smile; a hurried appearance; tightly crossed legs; a lot of nodding, followed by endless "uh huh's." Don't be discouraged, though. There will be another woman who will like and appreciate your efforts.

A woman wants to know you will be able to read her silent movements in the bedroom; being attentive when you first meet her is the perfect way to prove that when it comes to the language of the body, you're a gentleman and a scholar!

SEXUAL CHEMISTRY

We hear a lot about sexual chemistry—the urge or feeling that frequently brings two people together in the first place. What exactly is sexual chemistry and what's all the mystery? Actually, it's an impalpable element that exists between two people who are physically attracted to one another—a "hot" bonding.

I call sexual chemistry "juice"! If you don't have any juice for your lover, then you're in *big* trouble, because you'll always be looking over her shoulder at someone who does turn you on. And that's not a healthy situation. Let me give you a few examples of how this juice works:

Kathy, thirty-four, energetic, intelligent, and fun-loving, met Marty during his college stay in California: "From the moment I saw Marty, we both felt an over-powering sexual magnetism pulling us together. It was definitely primal. After college he went home to Paris, I followed. Twelve years later, we are married and have four kids. The first time we made love our sex was magnificent and now it's even better. But then again, we had the same sexual styles and communicated our desire and willingness to work toward the same goals."

Linda, thirty-two, filled with curious learning and bold opinions, works in a library. One day she was putting books away and she heard this melodious voice ask, "Excuse me, do you know where I can find Henry Miller's *Sexus, Nexus*, and *Plexus*? I found the *Tropics*, but not the trilogy." Linda immediately responded to his voice. She looked into his golden brown eyes and for some mysterious reason she couldn't speak. She tried again, "Uh, yes, someone returned them today. They've not been filed yet; they're on the counter. If you'll follow me . . ." Checking books in and out was not her job, but for this man, anything! After all, she needed time to think of some way to communicate. The desire to touch his face, inhale his aroma was overwhelming. To be close to him, to breathe in the same space, was a journey's end.

Some people will argue that sexual chemistry is instantaneous, physical, and purely primal; others will say it's a preexisting sexual fantasy that depends on a person's experiences and maturity; yet still others think it's a process of one's senses either accepting or eliminating the data they receive. The truth is it's all of the above. In a physical sense, it's animal magne-tism—the instant familiarity you can feel for someone is nothing short of pure magic. Chemistry is mental, too. You actually do walk around with a preexisting sexual fantasy in the recesses of your mind. In a millisecond your brain does an unconscious check—does she match up to my ideal fantasy? There's no doubt that sexual chemistry has *everything* to do with your senses. The moment you see her, you like what you see; when she comes close, you like what you smell; when she speaks, you like what you hear. From that first look, first sound, first smell, you're bonding. And if it continues, you bond through intercourse. Physically, you know she's the one. Later, if you stay together and fall in love, you'll have the best chance for a beautiful and lasting relationship.

The first step is to like *yourself.* You see, we reflect our needs, wants, and desires onto the other person. And by liking yourself, when you see your mirror image reflected back, *voilà*! Touchdown!

Remember, a positive attitude creates more positive sexual energy in a relationship, whereas negative energy can destroy your sexual drive altogether. So if it's lost and you both want it found, work together, communicate and rekindle the romance with all the thoughtful "little things."

2

· · · · · · · · · · · · · · · · · ·

What
Women
Want
. . . and
Don't

He who knows not and knows not he knows not;
he is a fool—shun him.

He who knows not and knows he knows not;
he is simple—teach him.

He who knows and knows not he knows;
he is asleep—wake him.

He who knows and knows he knows;
he is wise—follow him.

—ARABIAN PROVERB

R-E-S-P-E-C-T

The foundation of all good sex, as well as lasting relationships, is Respect. That is the first thing a woman desires from a man. It is the basis of all future trust and communication.

Every woman wants you to think that she's smart. If you ignore her intelligence, you are ignoring her. If you're interested in her mind as well as her body, I guarantee you will have an advantage over every other male vying for her attention.

But you must be completely honest in your respect; it must be genuine and come from the heart. If you're being real and she feels that, she will open herself up to you from her heart. Then watch things happen!

The gift of the self is the most precious gift you can bestow. Tell a woman how you truly think and feel. At the same time, be concerned, caring, courteous, and sensitive to a lady's needs and feelings. Don't nag, criticize, or try to make her over, and she'll open up to you in ways you never dreamed. If you've ever made love to a woman who trusts you completely, I don't need to tell you why it's important. After you've made her feel secure enough to let go, she'll experiment, expose, and express her innermost fantasies. Let her know that no matter what she does, you're not going to think of her as anything less than the apple of your eye. Never let her feel that you are judging her. A real man doesn't act as prosecutor, judge, or jury. That's bad news!

RESPECT IN WORDS AND DEEDS

Dependability. Start off on the right foot by keeping your word. If you tell her you'll call her at 4:00 P.M., be sure to call at 4:00 P.M. If you're unable to, let her know. She will appreciate the fact that you think her time is valuable, too.

When a man keeps his word consistently, a woman believes him just as consistently. When you need to change a date or rearrange an appointment, the woman will be understanding because you have already established a good track record.

Including her. When socializing with others, don't talk about business or old times unless your date can be included in the conversation. Squeezing her hand under the table, smiling at her a few times during the course of the evening, or making a few flattering comments does not mean you're including her in the conversation. Don't patronize or treat her in that condescending manner or she may do the same to you. Showing respect does not only mean saying the words "I love you, I respect you, I adore you"; it means acting respectfully, too. Include her not only in conversations but in other aspects of your life. Include her in some of your important decision making. For example, if you live in California and you're offered a big job in New York, ask her opinion. Include her in all areas that mean the most to you.

Her needs. Keep your presence felt in her life. Your lingering cologne, notes, phone calls, cards, a flower at her doorstep when she gets the morning paper, the book she mentioned that she'd like to read, tickets to a concert, stationery with her name on it, ideas you can give her that help her projects move forward. Try to remember things that are important to her, and ask how they turned out.

Anticipate her needs and wants. When you invite a woman to your home or apartment, you must have clean towels in the bathroom, no rings around the toilet or bathtub, an empty trash basket and plenty of toilet tissue and soap, clean sheets on the bed, a clean refrigerator well-stocked with fresh juice, soft drinks, mineral water, wine, or if you can afford it, champagne. If you are prepared, it tells her that you have thought about her in advance and were excited about her being in your home.

Don't take her for granted. Always respect a woman's efforts to please you, because believe me, it takes us a lot of time and attention to prepare for a special date. So the first time you see her, be sure to notice and compliment her dress, perfume, hairdo, nail polish, or jewelry, because she probably wore it especially for you. But remember, it must be genuine.

I was invited to the theater by a man I had considered "just a friend," until he picked me up in a limousine equipped with my favorite champagne and white roses. He wined and dined me, lacing the evening with timely compliments, which showed he noticed the preparation I had put into our date. Needless to say, I couldn't wait to be in his arms.

If a woman invites you to dinner in her home, remember that preparation of a meal is time consuming, and she has done this on top of making herself and her apartment immaculate for you. So eat with relish and take each bite enthusiastically. Pick up your plate, carry it into the kitchen, and ask if you can help with the dishes. Some men don't even ask—they just do it! She will adore you for appreciating her efforts, and will demonstrate it!

It's most important for a man to show respect for a woman's home and possessions. For example, if you happen to borrow her car, have it washed and/or filled with gas before you return it. If you can afford it, have it detailed, too. Perhaps you are unlucky and get a ticket. Pay it! If you borrow her records, tapes, CDs, or books, return them promptly and in good condition.

You can also show your woman respect by appreciating her desire to be alone sometimes. This shouldn't be a reason for you to feel left out or jealous. Actually, it's very healthy and quite normal; most secure people seek solitude from time to time. In the same way, sometimes she'll want to spend time with her family or friends. You should be pleased she has people around who love her. Be reasonable with your demands on her time.

Her mind. Prove that you're interested in your woman's mind, not just her body. Be mindful of her opinions; don't dismiss them if they differ from yours.

If she just got a promotion, take her out for a celebration. Let her know how happy you are for her by giving her a small present at the end of the meal. Warm rewards for you will follow. A woman needs to know that she's important and appreciated for her skills outside the relationship, too.

Women want to be taken seriously. No matter what you think of her job, to a woman her work is an expression of herself. If you put down her work, you put her down. Whether she has a nine-to-five job or does freelance work or something creative, have respect for where she puts her energies.

Respect her hopes and dreams for the future, whatever they are. If you are the man who helps her achieve her goals, you will be the man she'll do anything to please. Encourage her to share her wildest dreams with you—try to handle them and not get jealous! She may start talking about her dreams of the ideal lover or her fantasy "best-ever" sex. This may be her way of letting you know just what she wants. If you share your dreams with each other, that's communication, and those fantasies may just come true.

ROMANCE

Has your lovemaking fallen into a routine? Do you experiment and take each other to new heights of creativity and fun—or has your love life become very predictable? Do you roll over each other with joyous laughter afterward, or do you each say "ho-hum" and go to sleep?

What keeps every relationship fresh, alive, and vital is that special element of magic and mystery—we call it "romance." It's not something you can touch, smell, or see. It starts in the mind and begins to stir your emotions. It has no rules, and yet it defines your lovemaking more than you may know. It's all about living life and loving with abandon—with a sense of adventure, fun, and play. Let your imagination run free and begin to discover the delicious magic we call romance.

THE ESSENCE OF TRUE ROMANCE
The following excerpt from *Scarlett* by Alexandra Ripley describes how a woman feels when she's in love with a romantic man:

There was no cold, no rain, no weakness—only the burning of Rhett's lips on her lips, the heat of his hands on her body. And the power she felt under her fingers when she gripped his shoulders. And the pounding of her heart in her throat, the strong beat of his heart beneath her palms when she tangled her fingers in the thick curling hair on his chest. Yes! I did remember it, it wasn't a dream. Yes! This is the dark swirling that draws me in and closes out the world and makes me so alive, and free and spinning up to the heart of the sun.

"Yes!" she shouted again and again, meeting Rhett's passion with her own, *her demands the same as his.*

Romance is much like playing a game. It has elements of surprise, intrigue, fun, teasing, and breaking the rules:

"Smell my neck," whispered Rita, bringing Don's face down to her heaving breast. "Oh, no you don't," teased Don pulling away with a grin. "You've been a bad girl and need to be punished." Begging for mercy, Rita melted her body into his lap, searching for his fountain of forgiveness. Don quickly pulled her up and over his knees; he spanked her seductively, threw her onto the floor, cried wildly, and ravished her body and mind until she screamed! (This is a scene I invented!)

A man who is romantic plays his hand with confidence, anticipation, patience, and creativity, and is lavish in his dance of courtship. A woman will be very attracted to him because she will translate all of his romantic qualities to his future behavior in bed and beyond!

Throughout history men and women have played games using their imaginations to attract the opposite sex. As early as 4000 B.C., the Egyptians devised poems of great sensitivity and eroticism. Egyptian women beguiled men with lacquered and bleached hair, highly made-up faces, and intoxicating scents. The Egyptian men worshipped their women. In ancient Greek myths, the gods and goddesses wooed each other on the most grand and elaborate of scales. During the Middle Ages, knights romanced their "ladies of the green sleeves," and wooed them with music, gifts, and flattering words. Courtly love was born—and the long tradition began of worshipping women from afar. Women were idolized and put on pedestals. (This is actually rather a lonely place for a woman. Most would prefer to stand where they can reach a warm body!)

Today, some men still single out certain women for worship. Sure, a woman wants to be seen as the most beautiful in the eyes of the man she cares about, and wants to be treated differently from the rest. But she also wants real emotions and sincerity, not a place on a pedestal and isolation for all eternity. She wants to be on equal terms. She wants to go on the crusades with her hero, not be left behind.

All this boils down to sharing and involvement, which some women refer to as "commitment." How I *hate* that word, because in contemporary lingo, commitment—or any mention of it—is what sends both men and women packing. I'm sure you have seen the furor that word can create. Maybe we should change it to "connect." Let's *connect* to each other. Not bad. Maybe this word wouldn't trigger fears of intimacy, so we could forget self-imposed restrictions and limitations.

The claustrophic "c-word" is inappropriate for communicating feelings of both love and romance. Love is trust and understanding. Romance is many things, but basically it's carrying on a love affair—a joining together—a *connection*. Love is the ultimate feeling in everything we do with someone; romance is the itinerary to getting there.

So today, in other words, romance is really the *threshold* into a beautiful relationship.

Men who take time to romance a woman will always achieve their goal. A woman can be president of the United States, or own a chain of hotels or factories, but somewhere in her heart, she's still a little girl hoping that one day Prince Charming will ride up on his white horse and turn her world into Camelot. If a man can fulfill a woman's dream, she will turn into his reality and fantasy.

And, fellas, a woman will *always* test you, either consciously or subconsciously. When she suddenly loses her house keys or the car won't start or her stereo breaks or she has something heavy to carry . . . whether she knows it or not, she's reliving the age-old courtship dance. "Go slay a few dragons for me, baby!"

Romance is about creating an illusion out of the mundane. This is the basis of all miracles—taking the ordinary and transforming it. Every man can create his own aura of illusion. Some men use humor, others use paints, music, poetry, sports—whatever will evoke a woman's dreams. To be impressive, you must use your own particular talent to its fullest. Since your woman has a vivid imagination, stir her fantasy and a pumpkin can become a carriage, a rag a million-dollar ball gown, and you her "knight in shining armor."

LITTLE THINGS

Romance needn't mean expensive, lavish, or even much out of the ordinary. A romantic act can be simple; it's the *spirit behind the act* that will touch your beloved's heart. Giving a little gift that has personal significance can make all the difference. A single perfect rose of her favorite color will do, or a dollar's worth of her favorite candy, a particular incense, delicious smelling soap for her bath, a book that she would enjoy reading (perhaps some romantic poetry), a graceful vase, a simple trinket. It's all in the thought behind the gift.

You'll want to be sure to keep that special feeling alive even when you're not together. Pick up the phone and say hello—find out how her day is unfolding. If she's not there, leave a nice creative message with your most relaxed voice on her machine. Try reading her a line of your favorite poetry or sonnet. And, if you sing, sing her a song—she'll love you for it. Once in a while, there's the special charm of a wake-up call or a good-night call. (Know for sure what times will be welcomed. You don't want to incur her wrath, so learn if she's a night owl or if she likes to sleep in. She may just fall

asleep thinking of you, and invite you into her dreams.)
Be sure to mention her name often—women love to
hear their name coming from the lips of the man they
adore.

Music is essential to amplify a romantic mood and
will keep your presence lingering in her head long after
you're gone. Most women love audio tapes or music
boxes that play a favorite melody. A good idea might
be a set of harmonic wind chimes whose sounds linger
peacefully with every breeze. These musical threads
have long helped me relive the kiss, the touch, and the
smell of my man.

A whiff of a lovely fragrance can also remind you
of a particular person. Since the olfactory receptors are
among the most powerful of the senses, a sniff of your
loved one's cologne can often prompt a rise!

Letter writing may seem old-fashioned, but it's
quite romantic to most women. It's also revealing—a
useful way to find out more about someone, since people tend to write more easily what's truly on their minds
than saying it face to face. I met what I thought was
a fabulous man and asked him to write me a letter
when he went out of town, which he did. As I read it,
I thought, "My Lord, who in the world is this person?"
His outlook on life was nothing short of bizarre, cold,
angry, and confused. He hated his family and it seemed
as if he hated himself. On the other hand, I met a man
from a distant land and drooled over every word he
wrote. Because of his beautiful letters, I maintained a
long and cherished relationship with him.

Be yourself—just write whatever's on your mind.
The philosopher Jean-Jacques Rousseau said "To write
a good love letter you ought to begin without knowing
what you mean to say, and end without knowing what
you have said."

If you've tried and tried and just cannot seem to
write a letter, then I suggest a short note. Humorous,

romantic greeting cards can be endearing. Alternatively, you might send a telegram or card to her workplace that simply says, "Thinking of you." Every calendar month has a heart-warming day or holiday, be it Valentine's Day, Thanksgiving Day, Christmas, or Hanukkah. An unexpected card can make someone feel warm, festive, and uplifted. There are many occasions to make your loved one feel treasured. And don't *ever* forget her birthday or your anniversary!

Use your imagination to think of romantic ways to spend time with your beloved: a midnight swim, a walk on the beach, a drive in the mountains or along the ocean with the convertible top down. (If you don't own a convertible, try renting one for fun sometime.) Sitting in front of a crackling fire sipping wine or brandy is always a good bet. Don't forget walking in the rain holding hands, with or without an umbrella! Try afternoon tea at a charming, old-fashioned hotel. Or if you're lucky to be around museums, piers, and quaint shopping districts, by all means visit them.

Your lady may enjoy beer and pretzels under a tree in the park, or visiting your home where you can serve either cookies or biscuits and tea, or caviar or finger sandwiches with white wine or champagne. The food is not as important as the ambience. Let your charm and inventiveness always take center stage. And don't forget to surprise her, always surprise her. It creates mystery in romance. As you know, we women must have our mystery!

We love imagination and creativity in a man. It means he has "life in him," is quick on the trigger, and is ingenious. An imaginative man is always sexy, because in him lie infinite possibilities.

Another key element of romance is anticipation. The less we get, the more we want. Make her want you. In showing that you have the *desire* to touch her, you will excite her more than if you actually do it in the beginning of the relationship. There are ways of guiding a lady through a door, down a street, or corridor with a firm but gentle, "I'm in command" grip, preferably at the elbow, à la Fred Astaire gliding Ginger Rogers onto a ballroom floor. But don't make obvious excuses to touch her. Looking intensely at whatever body part catches your attention, then looking back into her eyes will definitely let her know that you like what you see, but will wait until the time is right to touch. Self-control always pays off.

Romance is about giving—giving yourself, your ideas, your time, your creativity, your innermost feelings, expressions from your heart. Romance is about men and women and the great heights we can reach together, with a little imagination.

ADVENTURES IN LOVE

Sex is about having fun and taking risks, so don't be afraid to let go and be creative! After all, how long can you do the ol' in and out? Get rid of the ordinary. Relax and be willing to make a fool of yourself. I'm not talking about whips, chains, and handcuffs; if that's your flavor, it's your business. I'm talking about trying something new and inventive for a few passionate moments. Put yourself in a state of inspiration. And remember, there's no such thing as can't. "Can't" is for a lazy man who won't try.

To make your romance dynamic and memorable or to rekindle an old flame, begin with a change of scenery or a mysterious surprise. Isn't it part of the male nature to be adventurous and pioneer new territories?

During my interview with Mandy, a sex therapist from Cleveland, we explored some of her wild adventures in graphic detail. She had been dating a man named Mike. Several months into their relationship, Mike phoned one day and asked her to go motorcycle riding. He told her he would pick her up at four in the afternoon and added, "Wear a dress and no panties!" Mandy told me her heart skipped a beat and, of course, she did exactly as he suggested. They set out for a secluded barn on the outskirts of town. On the way she experienced an orgasm from the vibrations of his engine and the closeness of his body. She couldn't resist her feminine urges, and started kissing his neck and dropping her hands from his waist down to his crotch. What they started on the bike was finished in the barn.

Sometimes it's sexy to seduce your woman without removing her clothes. (A word to the wise: in these days of heightened awareness regarding sexual harassment and date rape, you'd better make sure she wants to participate in your adventure.) Try a little variety. While having dinner in a restaurant, you could slip your hand up her dress as you compliment her loveliness with a sultry voice. She may resist or feel embarrassed, but don't let that stop you if you think she's just being coy. Advance slowly and persistently up her thigh until you reach something that makes her gasp and smile.

Do the same thing in a dark corner of a not-too-crowded movie theater or while waiting for the valet attendants to bring your car around. You might try your office desk while your clients are waiting in the next room or a secluded field when you're taking a walk. (Make sure you're alone and unseen.) It doesn't matter where you are, really; if you feel it's the right time, go for it. She won't be able to withstand her own passion.

For a special evening out with your woman, perhaps buy and giftwrap a garter belt, silk stockings, and erotic underwear. Women love things that feel silky or diaphanous. You might add some flowers and have them delivered with the package to her home. Include a little note asking her to wear the garments that night for dinner. (Little does she know that she will be the dinner!)

If you're feeling extravagant, rent a limousine and have a bottle of her favorite champagne on ice. Instruct the driver to stay on a straight road, avoiding curves, bumps, and excessive speed. Don't forget to raise the divider between you and the driver. (It's always rewarding to think ahead.) While riding, slowly remove her stockings and begin kissing every inch of her body, licking the bare flesh as it's revealed, but save her mouth for the finale and really kiss her lips like your tongue is an extension of your penis, which it should be.

Have you ever experienced phone sex? A lot of couples are enjoying it. Luke, a tax lawyer, revealed to me that he used to call 900 numbers for two dollars a minute to hear the forbidden fantasies of nymphomaniacs. He would listen to breathy, panting, nasty moans and groans while his girlfriend worked him over on his end. Luke said the experiences were interesting. He actually prefers phone sex with his own girlfriend. This allows them to stay in touch when they are on pressured schedules and unable to see one another. The phone serves as their sexual link. Always ask your woman first before trying phone sex with her. It's common courtesy, and besides, she might be appalled by the idea. You don't want to be embarrassed nor do you want to hurt her sensibilities. Make sure your woman feels passionate and secure with you before you take the initiative. Some women like it, others don't.

Many women have told me that swimming naked is a real turn-on because it's natural. The water is sensual in itself—and the feeling of skin on skin in water is even more delectable. Find a warm, safe lake and enjoy yourselves. Before you take the young lady swimming, make sure you are familiar with the area. You certainly don't want to be sucking on her breast while a water moccasin mistakes your erection for his dinner! For other aquatic variations, try making love under a waterfall—an especially exhilarating and adventurous experience.

Let me suggest some more adventurous places. Do you know Tina Turner's song "Steamy Windows"? It's about the pleasures of love at the drive-in. If you didn't do it in high school, it can be thrilling when you're an adult—like reliving your adolescence! And if you did do it in high school, it can bring back those crazy, libidinous days when every millimeter of your mind was filled with sexual seduction.

Even apartment- or house-hunting can turn into a sexy rendezvous. Make yourselves at home. Try out each room to see if you will be comfortable living there. Make sure the realtor is a safe distance away or they might think you're doing a *Last Tango in Paris* remake.

Ohhhhh! The airport! Try that one sometime. Watch planes take off and land while you're blasting off and coming down. But again, be discreet. You don't want to be interrupted when you're making love—it breaks the rhythm of the moment. (And, needless to say, you could be arrested.) If you love to fly, I've heard the "mile high" club has thousands of members. Whether in your seat on the "red eye," or in the matchbox-size restroom, I'm sure your fingers, at least, can be kept busy.

There is no greater high than being on a romantic adventure with your lover. When two people are in love, any place can be the right place, any time the right time. Lust will rear its head at the most unexpected moments. When this hunger engulfs you, reason takes flight, instinct takes over, and you find yourself acting out your deepest passions and wildest desires without inhibition.

Who you are as a man *is* who you are in bed. That's why life and sex flow into each other. To get, you have to give, and that includes passion. To please a lady you must be willing to go out on a limb. If you're afraid to take a risk, you'll miss all the fire a woman has to offer. So, let your heart and spirit soar!

TEASING

To tease is to please is the one concept most men don't understand. We want a slow hand. Nothing is more of a turn-on than good energy, the right timing, and an easy touch.

A woman wants self-control in a lover. Wait until she wants it as much as you do. Bringing us slowly to what we want sexually is the key to all female pleasure. Be patient and *wait* until she's delirious, craving and begging for you. And believe me, it won't be a secret. You'll know. A woman always lets a man know just what she wants him to know in many different ways. So pay close attention. You don't want to miss your cue!

The right touch is crucial to great lovemaking. You may think you know how to touch, but most men really don't. Just because a man gets laid—or says he does—all the time, doesn't mean he knows how to touch, especially if he announces, "Man, I really fucked her last night!" Then you know for sure it was a solo performance. He probably impaled her until she was missing several layers of skin. While he was thinking, "I'm a love stud," she was thinking, "He's a brute" and running her grocery list in her head while waiting for him to finish. To be a real stud, you need her un-divided attention.

The first time a man touches me often tells me all I need to know about his sensitivity. A man can take me by the arm and lead me into a dining room and I know instantly the way he will touch my body in bed. Call it our sixth sense. A woman can tell by looking at the way a man moves his hands and body, too. Remember, especially in the early stages of lovemaking, to be gentle and tender. A slow hand and an easy touch will dissolve any resistance she may have. A too hasty approach will make her tense and freeze, not to mention physically uncomfortable.

For your hands to become magic, your fingertips should be an extension of your mind. Your fingers alone can arouse, can make a woman's body tingle with divine pleasure and multiple orgasms, and can find their way into wonderful, strange places that your mouth or penis cannot. They can also be more subtle when exploring a woman's anatomical landmarks. The feelings your magic fingers can give the clitoris are sometimes more powerful than your thrusting penis.

While you learn about your woman's anatomy and her particular sensitivities, you will learn exactly how much pressure to apply and to which area. To get a sense of how to touch, put your hand on your stomach at the top of your pubic area. Let it rest quietly for a few minutes until you feel a certain warmth. Connect with your nerve endings. Energy will circulate as you press downward toward the pubic hair. Gently tug on your pubic hair. Now close your eyes and stroke the area with the pads of your fingertips as though they were feathers. Continue in a circular movement while your other hand travels slowly down your leg. After a few minutes, switch hands. Don't be afraid to explore your own body. It's healthy and will improve your dexterity and timing.

A woman will respond to certain locations more receptively than others. She will often guide you to the exact place or places she wants you to touch. Before you do all of this, you might want to put her in a nice bubble bath and bathe her from head to toe. When you begin your body feast, you will be certain that all areas are pristine. It's not unnatural to douche a woman. Some women find that quite erotic, when done by their lover or husband. However, there are some professionals who believe that douching is unhealthy and unnecessary. I believe that douching at certain times is both healthy and necessary.

There is no part of a woman's body that you can't explore with any part of your anatomy, and if you have skill and sensitivity, you can bring her endless hours of pleasure and fulfillment. The key is to spend some time—lots of time—and not come and go in a heated rush.

WHEN WOMEN WANT IT

You may think you're chasing the woman, but basically the woman is in control. She's the one who sets the pace and chooses the place. If you go to bed with her, it's because she chooses to surrender her mind and body at that particular moment. Mentally she was probably in bed with you long before you suspected she was interested.

You have everything to gain by letting the woman choose when and where. There are certain times when a woman gets really hot. She might throw you on a chair, sit on you, and do what she does best. If you've had this happen to you, deem yourself a lucky man. I'll bet you loved it. You see, we, too, are capable of unbridled, uncontrolled passion. A powerful urge sometimes takes over and we feel like Sheena, queen of the jungle. And when that happens, look out!

The kind of sex a woman craves will vary from day to day. Also, what becomes fun in a long-term relationship may not be that much fun on a first date. The special treat that worked unforgettably for both of you on her birthday might be exhausting if done every day.

To explain a woman's "hottest" times, her menstrual cycle must be accounted for. Don't feel alone if what you're about to learn surprises you. Many men are not aware of the following facts.

Ovulation is a two- or three-day window for fertilization. If you ejaculate or if your sperm meets her egg during these days, you will be changing diapers instead of changing sexual positions. Your sperm can remain fertile in her vagina for up to seventy-two hours, but most survive for about twenty-four hours. That's a long time, fellas. Fortunately or unfortunately, these two or three days of fertility can be the most erotic time for a woman. Her body is crying out for a mate. She may just unzip your pants and keep on going. At this time, you *must* use serious protection, at the very least a condom. (See chapter 4 for further discussion of condoms.)

Assuming a woman has a regular menstrual cycle of twenty-eight days, ovulation usually occurs within one day of the fourteenth day of the cycle. So from the twelfth to the sixteenth day, you are in *danger*. Some people avoid intercourse altogether for the four days prior to the day of ovulation and three days afterward. The shorter the cycle, the sooner ovulation occurs after her period. If a woman has a twenty-one day cycle or a thirty-eight day cycle, the day of ovulation (and therefore the period of "safety") can vary *greatly*. So to those of you guys who think you've got rhythm down—be careful!

There's another, safer time a woman can be animalistic sexually—the few days before her period begins. Unfortunately, certain women must cope with PMS (premenstrual syndrome). This can be a roller coaster ride of emotions and minor ailments, so you'll want to be on your best behavior. If you do make love to a woman when she's premenstrual, be extra gentle and understanding, because while she may want to have sex, she'll be dealing with other things as well.

Another erotic time is just after the period is over. A woman feels emotionally and psychologically safe from pregnancy. She feels free to relax and enjoy sex. "Where is he now?" she thinks. "Where's that Hunk of Heaven I want to devour?"

And if she's acting bitchy, ask yourself what time of the month it is. No matter who you date or who you're married to, you should make it your business to know where she is in her cycle and definitely when she ovulates. After all, it *is* your business if you're sleeping with her.

I've spoken to hundreds of men and asked them intimate questions about the female gender. I was shocked to discover that most men don't know very much about women's bodies in general, let alone the menstrual cycle. Billy Bob, a cute, hot country boy, asked Melba, a twenty-three-year-old blond from Shreveport, Louisiana, if she would go to bed with him. They'd been dating for a few months and he felt it was time. Melba politely refused, saying, "I can't, Billy Bob, I'm on my menstrual cycle!" Billy Bob's eyes lit up like neon signs and a big smile crossed his face. He responded excitedly, "Well, Melba, that's all right, I'm on my Honda, so I'll just follow you home!"

No one ever told Billy Bob about sex or women. What he knew he found out through trial and error. To avoid being like him, ask questions and read. You need to feed your curiosity, otherwise you will miss out on two of life's great wonders—feminine beauty and the joy of sex.

VIRGINS

I'm sure the following information isn't new to you. In fact, you probably haven't been in this situation for years. But I know this will ring a bell for everyone. I'm going to talk about the golden years, the early ones, when sex was brand new. When you, your partner, or both of you were virgins. The first time . . .

Betty June is the type of gal that both men and women love being around. She had the good fortune to meet Montgomery—the man who broke her hymen. "I was going steady with Monty for two years, when he formally asked my parents for my hand in marriage. They refused.

"One hot, humid Saturday night while I was in college, my parents left for a party. I had an exam the next day, so I went to sleep rather early, only to be awakened by a knock on my bedroom window. It was Monty. 'Betty June, let me in!' he whispered loudly. I opened the window. The wind glued my flimsy white nightgown to my sweaty body as Monty pulled me close with a heated embrace. He gathered my hair, pulling my head back while his mouth and tongue explored my neck and ears and whispering how much he loved me, how beautiful my body was, how he wanted to enter me slowly so I could feel him grow with love. He talked, cuddled, kissed, licked, and sucked. I was feeling wonderful when all of a sudden I felt a quick, sharp pain which turned into pleasure. We had been making love for hours when a car pulled up in the driveway—it was my parents. Montgomery scurried out the window the same way he entered, except with one difference: He took with him the sweet, musky memory of a virgin!"

Men, if you find yourself in this situation, remember that Monty made sure of two things when having sex with Betty June for the first time: One, she was appreciably lubricated with his slow, sensual timing, and two, he gave a single thrust with quick and deliberate propulsion once his head entered her vagina rather than a prolonged pressing and pushing which would have been considerably more painful.

Some virgins break their hymen while playing sports, riding bikes, riding horses, undergoing gynecological examinations, or even during masturbation. In those cases it wouldn't be so painful, if at all, during intercourse, but you should still be as sensitive—and reassure her that the pain is over and only good feelings will follow. You GUARANTEE it!

You must be aware that a young woman may be afraid of seeing your erection or being touched by it. Louise, a schoolgirl at Beverly Hills High, said she screamed the first time she saw a real penis. She had only seen pictures in magazines. One night her boyfriend, Peter, insisted that she play with it. "All the other girls are doing it," he said as he unzipped his pants and put Louise's hand on it. It wiggled, she screamed and fought desperately to escape the car carrying what she thought was a snake!

A golden rule: Don't force any woman—especially a virgin. Force and roughness could cause severe trauma to her emotionally and psychologically. It doesn't take an Einstein to figure out that kindness goes a long way. So do take care and treat her SPECIAL moment with respect. After all, it is a long-awaited celebration.

Most guys would do it parked on Fifth Avenue in New York City if they had the chance. But you must use discretion. You don't want to get caught in the middle of the act and traumatize the woman. A good suggestion is to take her to her home or yours, a motel, drive-in, friend's home, or brother's place when you know they won't be around. Wherever you take her, please make certain you will not be disturbed. This is not a time to stop and start. It needs a slow, flowing execution.

IF *YOU* ARE A VIRGIN

Ages ago, a father would take his son to his favorite bordello and pay his favorite "lady of the night" a handsome sum for the deflowering. In the nineties, this is ill-advised. If you've been waiting a long time to express yourself, my suggestion is find a compassionate, experienced woman. She will give you permission to be yourself, to explore your own sexuality and hers, to falter and then help you succeed. Providing you're lucky enough to seek out the right woman, you will bless her for the rest of your life—all your lovers will bless her too. Always be kind to the woman who gave you her yin to succor your yang!

Beware of the wrong woman. She may look terrific and seemingly have a nice nature, but when it comes to sex, she may turn from Dr. Jeckyll into Miss Hyde, so be advised: At the first sign of trouble, put on your shoes and make tracks. A bad experience can mar your attitude toward sex for a long time to come.

Most women will be kind during your passage into manhood, but you must be truthful. Innocence, sincerity, and confession are turn-ons. So don't affect a maturity that you haven't yet experienced. It will invariably turn to disaster. And besides, an experienced woman will always know, while a trusting girl will overlook your clumsy behavior if you're honest with her.

A word of caution here, guys: Don't deceive yourself into thinking that you have the power to pull out before you come; you *don't!* Or that a drop of your juice will not produce the miracle of life; it *will!* Or that once you come, it's all over, and reentering the vagina is okay; it's *not!* The pressure of reentry will cause several more tiny drops to squeeze out of your penis and impregnate her. Ignorance and bragging are the primary causes of unwanted pregnancies. And did you know that there are at least thirty kinds of STDs (sexually transmitted diseases)? These days, fellas, latex condoms are the best protection, other than abstinence, against venereal diseases and AIDS. Some men tell me that wearing a condom is like taking a shower with their clothes on. But this can be a turn-on too. As Batman described his latex apparel, "You gotta WORK THE SUIT, man!" So you put on your latex and work with it, whether you're with a virgin or an experienced woman. Then you can be safer against pregnancy and diseases. (See chapter 4 for a further discussion about condoms.) When you go through these landmarks of life, do it slowly. Don't rush, look around. Enjoy every moment. Give it the importance it deserves, because you won't be passing that way again. And remember, you're not alone. Other people are experiencing the same trepidations and the same expectations of happiness.

CLASSIC TURN-OFFS

If you have ever been halfway to home plate with your woman and something went wrong, then this section is for you. Here we begin to discuss the major turn-offs from a woman's point of view. Turn-offs are just as important as turn-ons.

EAGER BEAVERS

Some men are too eager to please. There's the bold type, who makes all the first moves without ever listening to her body language—or to her—because he's too busy declaring his admiration and bragging about the various ways he's going to please her to listen to what she wants. Wrong approach! You'll be talking to her answering machine more than you'll be talking to her.

Then there's the sensitive type, who's too worried about "performing" and insists upon a marathon every single time. That spoils the fun. Don't work at it so hard. This is your fun time, not your work time. Sex is not about impressing people, it's about enjoyment. Enjoy yourself!

Don't take your pants down like you're standing in front of an audience. No man can be good when he's under pressure to perform. Easy does it is the key. When you feel at ease, you'll make her feel at ease. She doesn't want to be made love to as if you're trying to win a competition. Just be yourself. In fact, both of you should allow the other to be yourselves.

PLAYING ROUGH

Big turn-off! Don't be too rough, even with women who like it. There's a time and place for roughness. Although some women actually prefer this type of expression of forcefulness, it has to be exactly the right time. Generally, however, most women really appreciate patience and delicacy.

Even the biggest and strongest men can have the most gentle hands and sensitive touch. I consider John Goodman a big, strong man, don't you? He was sitting in front of me with his wife and child on the plane going to New Orleans. I was privileged to watch for many hours how gently and delicately he played with his baby and how lovingly he responded to his wife. He's definitely a big man with a sensitive touch.

And guys, *never* hit a woman. I couldn't believe how many of the women I interviewed told stories of being hit by men. No wonder you've got a bad reputation with some people! If you're that frustrated, you must deal with your problem—not take it out on others. I consider a man that defines his "manliness" by hitting women to be the lowest of the low. "All cruelty springs from weakness," observed the Roman philosopher Seneca.

TIMING

As you know by now, timing is everything. Some men use a moment when a woman is vulnerable, like when she's crying over a sad ending to a movie, to make their move. Hold it, fellas! *Bad timing!* She might think you're an insensitive lout and that will be the end of you. Instead, take her hand and in a soft, soothing voice, discuss why she was so moved. Slowly and deliberately wipe her tears away, then hold her gently in your arms until she has quieted down. Lift her chin sweetly and brush your lips across her lips, her wet eyes, and her face. If she responds, you'll know what to do next.

Most women I know don't like it when you ask permission. It's like raising your hand in school and asking to go to the bathroom. Never ask if you can kiss her—it shows you can't read her signals and kills the romantic moment. Instead, communicate with your eyes, moving your face closer to see if she's ready. So read the situation, take a risk, and be a gentleman if your efforts fail. There'll be another time, another place.

MR. MANNERS

You'll gain more yardage by being considerate rather than not. If she's trying to lose weight, don't suggest eating a hot fudge sundae because you want one—make it frozen yogurt, at least. If she tells you she has a big day tomorrow, don't keep her out all night for your own pleasure, because when the morning comes, she's going to hate you for those bags under her eyes.

THE BIG ONE

Never do any of the following things: enter her apartment, turn on the TV, and say you'll just watch it until they announce the score; refuse to be in the same room as her pet; take your shoes off, put your feet on the coffee table and wait to be served; ask her to fix you a sandwich and tell her all the things you want on it; invite her back to your place to watch a movie on your VCR and not tell her until it starts that it's a porno film; boss her in lovemaking as though you were a movie director; tell your girlfriend how gorgeous she is, then say how she reminds you of your ex-girlfriend; brag about how much money you make (you should never do this anyway) and ask her to pay for dinner because you forgot your cash; complain about the price of movies and parking tickets as you usher her into an expensive restaurant—you'll appear cheap; send your dinner back while being rude to the waiters—it's not their fault; complain that women always try to rope you into marriage—this is stupid and will lead to eternal bachelorhood; try to appear smart by talking about subjects or using words you don't fully understand—you'll look really dumb!

Finally, don't maul her or slobber all over her when you arrive to pick her up or when out on a date. She has probably spent a long time on her hair, makeup, and clothes. The idea is to admire them, not manipulate them. Hold her hand, if she lets you. A peck on the cheek or neck may be appropriate, but that's all . . . for the moment! And don't put your hand on her leg to try and show ownership in the company of friends. It's ill-mannered, insecure, and repulsive to a woman, especially if you only just met her. If you want your woman to be all that you dream, then you must first be the gentleman she dreams about!

COLLECTING STAMPS OR
HOW TO GET DUMPED

Every woman has what I call a hypothetical "book of stamps." This is an especially valuable principle for you to understand, because it explains, once and for all, why we can suddenly become so angry for no apparent reason.

Here's a classic stamp-collecting story. You have a date with a wonderful woman next Saturday night. You're excited about her and she's thrilled about you. This means she'll spend a lot of time, effort, and money preparing for your date.

You pick her up and go to dinner. The food is delicious, the wine excellent, the conversation delightful, and passion on the rise. So far everything is lovely and romantic. You brush a single hair from her face as you look deep into her eyes. She gently touches your arm in conversation. You laugh, you ask questions, you're curious about her work, you flirt, you tease. You pay the check. She's impressed with your generosity and your treatment of the waiters. You pull her chair out, open all her doors. The drive home is fun, a little silly and filled with laughter. You feel like you've known each other forever or in some past life. She can't take her eyes off you in the dark. As you get out of the car and walk to her door she "accidentally" finds a way to touch some part of you and feels your taut muscles. She fumbles with the key. You take it from her hand and open the door. You thank her for a lovely evening and make the motion to leave. She stops you, "Won't you come in for a brandy?" You accept with glee!

She turns on sultry saxophone music and serves the brandy. You clink glasses with a toast as you look directly into each other's eyes. Your bodies shudder with want. You sip your brandy, eyes completely transfixed. You put your glass down and urgently pull her to you. Your burning lips find her wet, open mouth. They touch and ignite. You're both delirious, dizzy with desire. The longer you kiss, the deeper your passion grows. Beautiful, slow foreplay begins.

OK guys, this is the moment that separates the men from the boys. She's hot, she's wanting, she's pulling your clothes off, she's touching you all over. You're happening, you're hot—and all you can think about is *entry*. You slide it in and a few seconds later, you *blow*—the whole evening! Boy, what a letdown. Now, you *may* think you did the ol' in and out for quite a while. But the ol' in and out didn't come close to satisfying that beautiful creature who spent half her salary and many hours preparing for her dessert . . . *you!* You so aptly fed her, but you didn't let her finish— you didn't let her orgasm. Big mistake!

You both put your clothes on, turn the lights back on. You sit on the couch drinking a little more brandy before you leave. She shuts the door behind you and guess what she thinks? I don't even want to tell you!

She walks into her bedroom and while getting ready for bed, she puts one stamp in her make-believe "book of stamps." This woman doesn't know she has a book of stamps. But every time you do something that leaves her empty, frustrated, angry, or unfulfilled, another stamp goes into her book.

Now you've been dating for a while. You think

everything is copacetic. She's happy too. But one day you call to break an engagement in favor of going to a Dodger game because your buddy scored great seats. You should go when you have great seats, nothing's wrong with that. But, what she thinks is, You say you're going to see her when you don't, and you say you're not going to ejaculate when you do! The point is, when you let your beautiful woman down time and time again, even in trivial ways, the frustration accumulates. Are you getting the picture?

After a while, your woman will become accustomed to all your excuses and little hurts until . . . you're in the kitchen pouring a cup of hot coffee, you miss the cup, and the coffee spills all over her freshly waxed floor. And *look out!* She goes off in twelve languages, none of which you understand, except the familiar four-letter English words which are reserved exclusively for such special occasions!

There you are, little innocent you, standing there feeling like a fool, saying "But what did I do? What did I do?" What you did has been recorded in the stamp book, page after page after page. Now you may think "All right, I'll clear it up—no problem, right?" *Wrong.* Dead wrong. Here's the deal: You know all those times you made love and she never had an orgasm? All the times you said you were going to take her somewhere and something more pressing came up? All the times you insisted she dress to the nines for an office party, because the possibility of a promotion was imminent? It could be any number of events that misfired leaving her sitting at home, alone—and seething. Perhaps it was that Christmas party she was so excited about going to, until you left her alone in a corner while you went off to meet interesting people—especially women—without her, pretending it was a social obligation. You see, all these minor incidents become an imaginary book of stamps—but it's all real to her.

She didn't care about the floor or the coffee. She exploded because her book of stamps was *full*. That's the reason most men do not understand most women. You think we're all crazy because most of the time we appear to not act logically. You need to understand that to us we make perfect sense. I've always wanted to explain this to men when I see them looking quizzically as if, "What the hell did I do *now?*" Just remember it's never one thing. It's a bunch of little things strung together.

To avoid this situation, start communicating. I can't stress enough that you need to read her silent signals. Keep your word, don't criticize or take her for granted. She's there because she wants to be with you, with all her heart and soul. Communicate both in and out of the bedroom, so you can be sure of giving your woman total satisfaction. After you do, loving you will become one of the most important parts of her life.

3

....

*How
to Get
Started*

*Happiness is the only good.
The place to be happy is here,
The time to be happy is now,
The way to be happy is to make others so.*
—ROBERT G. INGERSOLL

WOMEN MEN WANT TO AVOID

*A woman drove me to drink and
I never even had the courtesy to thank her!*
—W. C. FIELDS

It has always been women who have chosen men. They look for husbands who are good providers and fathers, but men are unaware of this; they think they are doing the choosing. This leads to all kinds of trouble, because they never bother to question why a woman says yes.

Misreading a woman can be disastrous. I'm talking about the kind of woman who acts like she's mad for you, when in truth she is conniving to ensnare you for reasons other than true love. Her well-developed and highly effective methods play on your egos and insecurities.

A word to the wise: No matter how smitten you are with a woman's beauty or supposed innocence, if she ever feigns a God-like worship of you and pretends you are in charge, go out for a paper one night and never come back! She might be capable of roping you into supporting her whole family. I've seen this happen many times. As a matter of fact, twice to the same man!

Here are some of the classic types of behavior to watch out for. They're all based on women I have known. You may have known some of them too.

SHERYL SHARE-ALL

The bulge Sheryl's interested in isn't the one in your pants—it's your bank account. So if you don't have money, prestige, or power, Sheryl isn't interested. However, if you do, or your family does, look out. She's on a mission to take all you've got. She'll become the IRS, the FBI, and the CIA rolled into one.

In the beginning, you'll think Sheryl is your dream come true. Every waking moment she's trying to please you. Sheryl usually:

— has a good body, face, or mind and knows how to use them
— has large silicone breasts—and pretends they're real!
— plays hard to get at first
— fakes orgasms, a lot
— constantly tells you what a great lover you are, how fulfilled she is with you, how she never even had an orgasm until you
— always asks you what she can do to please you, in bed or out
— learns to cook your favorite foods
— runs your errands, and tends to your every private need
— digs up the intimate details of your life
— gets very close to your friends and family
— has lunch with your mother, takes your kids to the zoo
— wants you to get close to her parents and siblings
— finds out your weaknesses quickly and uses them to her advantage
— demands you tell her everything, but tells you nothing

In the beginning, it's "she does, she does." But once she's reeled you in, it will be "you do, you do," until you're in misery. That is when she'll begin to badger you to take her to Europe, buy her a new car, or put money up for her own restaurant, boutique, or public-relations business. Marriage will become a huge issue at this point. In fact, all of this was designed to get you to marry her.

If you don't get on with her program fast enough, she'll begin the emotional blackmail. This will take many forms, but the message is always the same: Look at everything I do for you, I gave up my career, the best years of my life, and my friends, and now *you owe me*. In the worst-case scenario, she'll get "accidentally" pregnant. If she has this child, she will use it to wheedle what she wants from you for the rest of your life.

Some of the men who end up with Sheryl just want to be stroked, have everything their way, and have their needs met—they will eat well, live in comfort, and have their sexual needs fulfilled regularly by a woman who looks good. They can't even tell when she's faking an orgasm, because they're so concerned with their own pleasure and greatness.

Never be too busy or impatient to find out all you can about a woman you desire. Any man who himself has a need to give in return or to nurture a two-way relationship, would quickly see through a woman like Sheryl. All a man has to do is wake up and realize a relationship requires equal participation. That means *you!* You must lead as well as be led.

Here are some other classic characters to beware of:

SHE'LL-HAVE-YOUR-BABY SHEILA

— has no motivation; is even lazy
— doesn't want a career
— goes after men with money
— wants security and protection

— is the homey type
— sticks around you and the house
— is legitimately boring
— stays put once she achieves her goal
— usually has a good figure
— loses her figure after marriage or becomes neurotic and extremely thin
— wants everything, gives nothing
— is a hypochondriac
— is always pretending, especially orgasms

HELL-BENT HILDA

— is extremely intelligent
— is ambitious social climber
— has achieved a lot professionally
— wants to be President
— finds her husband in an extramarital affair, uses it to further her goals
— retains extraordinary influence over her husband's career
— superior manipulator, incredibly cunning with a "mighty mouth"
— moves willfully on her way to destruction
— redefines her character to whatever suits the moment
— can cook when necessary
— is good in bed when she wants something
— considers herself attractive
— pretends to be a good mother for the sake of public image

HIGH-MAINTENANCE HELEN

— thinks she always deserves the best
— thinks she's beautiful and can't spend enough on her appearance

— demands a lot, and if you don't give, you're history
— acts secure and on top of things at all times
— is allergic to work
— may do without early on but will put the screws in later
— expects you to kiss her feet; walks if you don't
— is spoiled rotten; wants it all on a silver platter

BETTER-DEAL BETTY

— is very pretty
— seeks adventure
— has a short attention span
— is self-motivated
— is career-motivated
— is opportunistic, social climbing
— goes to the highest bidder

CONNIE THE CONNIVER

— is very attractive and knows it
— is straightforward: makes clear-cut sex-for-service deals
— sleeps her way to the top of her career
— uses her body as a credit card

TAMARA THE TROPHY-CATCHER

— wants the satisfaction of conquering
— makes love, shares a home, has children—all for ego gratification
— often gets accomplished men to father her children
— is good looking, strong willed, and successful

A lot of men told me they each dated at least one woman who, the first week, left her shoes, the second week a few dresses and a robe, the third week she took over a drawer, and a month later, filled the closet with her belongings and the bed with herself. They can't get the woman to move out, because she has nowhere to go. She has no money, and guess what? She's lost her job and she just wants to stay a few more weeks until she finds another job. Which, of course, she never does.

The way to keep these women from ruining your life is, first, not to kid yourself. Know who you are and don't let her play you up to be the man you *wish* you were—the greatest lover who's the smartest, funniest, handsomest catch around. Second, don't let her get away with being less than she can be by latching onto you. Only when both of you are complete as individuals will you have any kind of satisfying relationship together.

THE PERFECT WOMAN

A good lover is a good reader of women. He knows that a walk in the rain may excite some women enough to rip off their clothing and run naked and dance with abandon, while others will sneeze, cough, and cling to him with discomfort. He knows how to please different types, but also knows what type of woman will please him. If you like hiking in the mountains, don't choose a woman who feels uncomfortable without her sunglasses, perfume, and stockings.

Only you will be able to distinguish the differences among the women you are dating by the signs they give; obviously, you'll need to read between the lines. Signs vary from the clothes she wears, the way she decorates her home, the way she walks and carries herself, her mannerisms, a nod of approval, or a twinkle in her eyes. If you *listen* and *notice* these signs, you'll understand a great deal about your woman, right from the start, and know if she's your type.

To know if a woman is right for you, you'll have to take an active role in your relationships. Probe the woman's feelings the same way she probes yours. Get to know her: Find out where she came from, where she's been, what she wants out of life, her values, her friends and family, her education, her job, her secrets and fantasies. Know everything that is humanly possible to know about the woman you desire. It's natural to be curious, and it's the sign of a sharp mind. A woman will also be flattered by your interest.

If you just settle for any woman who will go to bed with you, you're settling for a fraction of the potential pleasures life has to offer, not to mention exposing yourself to the dangers to your health by being indiscriminate! No one really respects or loves an easy lay. When you get in quick, you get out quick. Easy come, easy go. You must work to get anything worthwhile, in business and in relationships. When you know you were thoughtful and worked hard for what you've got, you will be able to enjoy it more.

You should notice all women's cultural differences. Of course all women are unique individuals, but we can be categorized into basic types. If you've been restricting yourself to one or two types of women, and you haven't been successful, you might try widening the playing field.

Take into account, for example, the region she's from. You can save a lot of time and heartache by treating a woman appropriately based on her cultural or ethnic background. Know that if she has one characteristic, she'll probably have another that goes with it. She'll appreciate the effort.

The following guidelines are only a way to start understanding her. They can remind you what questions to ask yourself. But remember, *no two women are alike!* That's half the fun of the courtship game!

MISSISSIPPI MAMA

Soft-spoken and honey-tongued, this gal was taught to please her man at an early age. Usually very hot in bed. Acts delicate and submissive, has mastered the art of feminine persuasion, will often cry, is gracious, charming, and socially adept, has old-fashioned values, is family oriented. Can be manipulative. (Example: Scarlett O'Hara in *Gone With the Wind*.)

NEW YORK NANCY

Career driven, no nonsense, hasn't much leisure time, is cultured, smart, quick, determined, aggressive, a little rough around the edges from competing with men in a man's world. Can be defensive. (Example: Lois Lane in *Superman*.)

MIDWESTERN MELANIE

Direct, frank, and aboveboard, freshly scrubbed, forthright, honest, self-motivated, driven, often has passionate causes. Can be stubborn and unbending. (Example: Mary Baily in *It's a Wonderful Life*.)

TEXAS TAMMY

Ambitious, pioneer-type woman, usually sportsminded, loves the desert, countryside, outdoors, is strong and sturdy, a good homemaker, reliable, independent, not afraid of anything. Can be a social climber and position seeker. (Example: Jacy Farrow in *The Last Picture Show*.)

NORA NORTHWESTERN

Culture oriented, has a sharp mind, is analytical, is a work in progress, needs constant change, keeps up with the latest trends, reads books on modern relationships or the current fad, is attached to her home ground to the point of being inflexible. Independent. Can be frosty. (Example: Maggie O'Connell in *Northern Exposure*.)

HOLLY HOLLYWOOD

Social climber, fun-loving, anything goes, materialistic, opportunistic, nutritionally careful and fad oriented, driven, is a daydreamer, wants to be a star, might ask, "What kind of car do you drive?" before she asks your name. Will buy into any situation at the risk of endangering herself. Can be gullible. (Example: Any woman in a Jackie Collins novel.)

Lastly, of course, there's the woman of your dreams. The perfect woman every man would choose if he could. She's your private incarnation of pleasure.

IDA IDEAL

The following are qualities to look for. You may not find them all in one woman, but if you're lucky, the woman you fall in love with will possess many of these superb characteristics:

Loves life, and loves you, has a great sense of humor, she makes you happy when you're sad, she massages your feet when you're tired, she feeds you when you're hungry, she heals you when you're sick, she'll do you when you're horny, in bed she's a whore and out of bed she's a lady. She's a wonderful mother, hostess, and homemaker, is successful in her job, is stimulating, wise and thoughtful, she loves people, children, and animals, she takes care of her body, feeds her mind, and nurtures her soul, she loves music, dance, art, travel, food and wine, and is resourceful and adventurous. She loves romance, knows how to turn your weaknesses into strengths, is always supportive, never critical, is honest to a fault, ambitious but never overbearing, quick-witted but never sharp-tongued, strong-willed and decisive yet sensitive and vulnerable. She loves being a woman and loves that you're a man!

Whoooooee! Sounds pretty good, no? Where do we find her? To get an Ida, you've got to be prepared to be her male equivalent . . . that's the key! To get what you want, you have to be ready to give the same.

GREAT PLACES TO MEET WOMEN

Many men have asked me, "Where can I meet a good woman?" I feel the best time to meet the opposite sex is while you're doing something that interests you. That way, you're sure to have at least one thing in common! Do what you like doing best, or expand into areas you'd like to know more about. Here is a list of places to go or things to do to spark your imagination:

— Art gallery openings and exhibits. A lot of women are interested in art. It's cultural, it's beautiful, it's fun.
— A gym. But don't interrupt her workout. Smile at her or catch her eye as she's leaving or coming in.
— A party. If you never get invited to parties, give your own. Invite single friends and couples, and ask them to bring friends.
— Sports. Trips or adventures, like white-water rafting or hang-gliding might not be available to everyone. But there's nothing to stop you from joining the local tennis or golf club.
— Walking your dog is always a great conversation starter.
— The beach.
— Sushi bars. Japanese food is about sensuality and

spontaneity. Sushi bars are full of relaxed, fun people enjoying themselves.

— Friends of friends. Your women friends would probably like nothing more than to set you up with one of their friends. Many of us are matchmakers at heart. The risk—you hate each other instantly, creating an awkward situation for the mutual friend—is usually worth taking. To some extent, you can pre-screen the women before deciding whether to meet them by finding out as much as possible about them from your friends.

— Political/environmental organizations.

— Club meetings, such as motorcycles, photography, or skiing.

— Alcoholics, Overeaters, or Debtors Anonymous.

— A library or museum.

— Stores. Bookstores are good places to inspire conversation. In department stores women are always eager to help you poor shy men buy something for your mothers.

— A record store. A fine place to discover a girl who dances to your beat.

— The elevator at work, or the water cooler.

— Acting classes or theater groups. They're full of beautiful women with active imaginations and fantasy lives.

— A dancing, martial arts, or yoga class. I teach beginning ballet and you wouldn't believe the gorgeous, graceful creatures at the barre. And they're all clad in skimpy leotards!

— Church. There's a lot of activity going on at the church of your faith. Join in!

— Cooking- or kitchen-supply stores. Many women are interested in gourmet cooking. Maybe you could recommend the best knives for cutting. Share your knowledge—it would be appreciated.

— Health-food stores. Women who are into their bod-

ies and health usually shop there. If you're a
healthy sort of guy, you're sure to meet a healthy
sort of gal.
— Movie memorabilia shops. You're sure to find a
woman who appreciates the old black-and-white
films and probably knows a lot about them. A
movie buff, so to speak.
— Walking in malls. A lot of people can't afford much
these days, so they simply stroll and window-
shop.
— Hobby stores. Most people have at least one hobby.
If you don't have one and want to meet a woman,
take one up that fits your personality. Stamp collecting, coin collecting, rare-book collecting. Col-
lectors are usually fanatics, so it will be easy
conversation.
— Flea markets. You'll see a variety of people at any
flea market.

HOW TO KNOW IF A WOMAN IS INTERESTED

If you're always looking below her neckline or at her
backside, how are you going to know what kind of
woman she is? Watch her closely. Observe her body
language. Look at her face, see how she responds to
different things people are saying. Does her face change
when she looks at you? Does her behavior change when
she's in your presence? I've already introduced you to
body language earlier in the book, but it's a crucial
lesson that's well worth repeating.

BODY LANGUAGE—THE ADVANCED CLASS
I can't emphasize enough the importance of eyes. If
you observe closely, a woman's eyes can tell you just
about everything you need to know. Her eyes may be
telling you one thing while her mouth is telling you

another. Everything she needs to express, she'll say with her eyes: You will see when she's angry, when she's sick, when she's sad, when she's happy, when she's pleased, when she's aroused. You will know when she wants to make sweet love to you or be left entirely alone. Eyes never lie! (Make sure she's not a professional gambler. You'll never read those eyes.)

The following are some key signs to look for that usually mean she's interested:

— She looks directly into your eyes.
— She engages you in some way.
— She smiles her million-dollar smile.
— She wets her lips or runs her tongue over her teeth.
— She unconsciously fondles her glass.
— She touches her hair, face, or other body part in a seductive, caressing way.
— She touches you.
— If you move closer she doesn't move away.
— Her voice level changes. If it's normally soft, it may rise. If it's low, it may get even lower. Or it may go up and down. In any case, a sensuous or changing voice means she's probably interested. Listen to the "music."
— She shops for groceries at the store you frequent, even though she doesn't live in the area.
— If she sleeps with you on the first date—she's foolish, but she likes you.

Sometimes a woman just isn't interested, period, no matter what you do or say. Many men are caught up with their own egos and persevere, refusing to acknowledge the woman's "Don't get mad, but please *go away!*" signals. There wouldn't be a problem with this, except that some men make the mistake of misreading signals that mean a woman doesn't want to hurt your feelings. They just want you to like them—but that's all!

If she is saying pleasant things to you, but something doesn't feel right, these early warning signals should tell you she's *not* interested:

— The conversation has been pleasant, but she doesn't leave you an opening to call.
— She flirts with you interminably, is extremely confident in the flirtation, but is never available for a date. She's always tied up with one thing or another.
— You both leave a place at the same time, and she waves good-bye and hurries off.
— She gives you her phone number, you ask her out twice, and she can't go.
— You call several times and she doesn't return your phone calls.
— If she goes out with you but doesn't sleep with you after a few months, or even eight or ten dates, she's either a virgin, very religious, or looking for a big brother and not a lover.

So, men, learn to read and hear women's language. You will need patience, perseverance, understanding, and the ability to accept rejection. You will need to use all *six* of your senses.

TIPS FOR THE FIRST DATE

I asked the women I interviewed what was an ideal first date. My statuesque, blonde friend Lana, a winner of ten beauty titles, said that she prefers to be wined and dined at a nice restaurant with a down-to-earth guy. She loves it if he sends her roses, but to bring a single rose is very special indeed. She absolutely hates it when a man puts on an act or talks about himself all night. But she doesn't like a man who won't talk at all. Lana said she loves curiosity in a man. After dinner, she enjoys going somewhere with a good view to relax and talk some more.

Patty, a sparkling blue-eyed brunette with the greatest face and body I've ever seen, is mostly vegetarian, and she appreciates it when a man takes this into consideration when they dine. She hates dancing, so if a man tries to surprise her and take her dancing without warning her, the date is always a disaster. What she dislikes most is that awkward moment when a man tries to kiss her on a first date. She likes a man who knows how to wait and doesn't rush her.

Green-eyed, twenty-two-year-old Dana, who works in advertising, said she likes a first date to be mysterious. She wants the man to carefully plan the whole evening and surprise her by taking her to interesting or scenic places. She hates it when a man comes on too strong too soon. Only if things are going well, she says, can she loosen up and "get crazy." She likes to have dinner, take a ride, go dancing, and walk on the beach. She may want to cuddle, but nothing more until future dates. If her date is sympathetic and listens when she speaks, she can't wait to see him again.

I've cited these three examples because I don't know any man alive who wouldn't give up fifty-yard-line Super Bowl tickets to take just one of them out. They're young, lovely, ravishing creatures with brains, style, and humor. That's why they always have men waiting in line. The point is that it is not difficult to please them and to get intimate with them *if* you pay attention to their particular needs. Then they will pay attention to yours.

Try to make the place you're taking her a fifteen-minute drive, more or less, from her house. That's generally long enough to take her out of her same old neighborhood, but not so long that the drive will put her to sleep. Get somewhere fast; maybe she had a hard day and forgot to eat.

If you happen to meet her friends or her room-mate, make them like you. Remember their names, be attentive and a little spunky, but never come on to them. She'll be asking them for their opinions about you, and you'll want to shine.

Be attentive to what your date likes so the next time you go out with her you'll know better where to take her. It's very impressive when a man notices all those little things that mean a lot.

To get a second date, the first date should not generate any bad feelings. It should be mysterious, have a few harmless surprises, no loud music, and a lot of talking. All of the women said they want to talk—it can be an aphrodisiac. You can talk your way into a woman's heart, if you're sincere. A lot of information must pass between you, but your first date should be light, unless you've known her for some time. No gypsy violins unless the passion has been building. Think what you'd like her to tell her friends about you.

TO KISS OR NOT TO KISS

There's always a first time. For kissing, this time often happens on the first date, which is why it's so crucial —it could cement the start of something wonderful, or it could blow the whole relationship.

When you take her home after your first date, do you kiss her? If you've been having a wonderful con-versation, you've been looking into her eyes, and she's been looking into yours, I don't think there is anything wrong with kissing her goodnight. There's a kind of sexual energy that comes out of good conversation, an up, positive, exciting feeling. If that feeling is there, go for it. Women love to kiss, especially when they are turned on to the guy.

Start slowly. Pull her firmly but gently toward you. Touch her face, look in her eyes, and begin planting tiny, delicate kisses first on her lips, and then on various parts of her face, especially the eyelids and ears.

Run your fingers over her lips. Then kiss her again on the mouth. When you kiss her, kiss her with deliberate intent—don't hesitate. And don't ask her first—her eyes will tell you. If she's a little reticent, kiss her with your mouth slightly open, without using your tongue; it's warm, lingering, and sensual.

After the kiss, *stop!* Kiss her gently on the eyes, forehead, or tip of the nose and say, "Goodnight. I had a wonderful time, and I can't wait to see you again." It's good to leave a woman turned on. A goodnight kiss should be one of rising passion, that you stop not because you don't want to go any further, but because you want to have that beautiful, sensual moment linger. It shows that you have respect for her, and that you have self-control. Now there's so much to look forward to.

For the same reasons, you might want to avoid kissing her altogether on the first date. Wondering what you kiss like, what you taste like, what your tongue feels like, may be more enticing to a woman than actually kissing. If you don't kiss her after a great evening, it'll make her crazy for you. She'll be thinking about your eyes, your voice, every single thing you've said, the way you smelled, how generous you were, how charming, attentive, and affectionate . . . and she will be waiting for your call.

When you take a woman home after a date, and get to the door, she may invite you in. This is usually an indication that she wants more than a goodnight kiss. But don't assume you've got carte blanche to do what you like—she's just showing you it *could* happen, not that it *will*.

So don't take liberties once inside the door, but don't revert to the formality when you fetched her three hours earlier, either. Just enter her home and make yourself comfortable. Relax. If she offers you something to drink, accept it and keep your eyes on her, letting her know you're excited, interested, turned on. Smile, keep that twinkle in your eyes, and notice the painting or pictures on her wall, her pets, her plants. She may excuse herself and come back with something sexy on. That's still not an indication that she's willing to have sex with you on the first date. It might just mean that she wants to kiss and cuddle. Exercise control, gentlemen. It's more manly.

Kissing is so exciting for women. If you're a good kisser, the woman you're with may just want to kiss for a long while and feel your body warmth next to her. Kiss all the areas you can visibly see until you get the green light to get down. Kissing her neck is one of the most exciting things you can do with your lips short of more serious foreplay. Her collarbone is a sensual place to kiss, or her hands, the inside of her elbow, her wrist, her fingers. Be tender but deliberate. A woman likes to know that a man knows what he is doing.

If you're kissing her right, she will feel very sexy. Don't try to eat her up and devour her as though you hadn't eaten food for two weeks. And while you're kissing, don't feel her up or try to pull her clothes off. The flavor and thrill of the kiss should take all your concentration. Notice what excites her.

No matter how much you may want to make love to her on this first date, my advice is *don't!* Pull yourself together and say, "I really must go, and it's not because I have to get up early in the morning. It's because if I stay any longer, I'm going to try to take advantage of you and I want to see you again and again. I don't want this to be just a one-night stand." This is exciting to a woman; if you've been aroused and she can feel that, it's even more exciting. Knowing that you want her that badly is a gigantic turn-on.

And guys, whenever you kiss, kiss as though it's the first time, *every* time.

HOW TO WINE AND DINE

A good dinner sharpens wit, while it softens the heart!
—JOHN DORAN

In my experience, a man who can appreciate the delights of a delicious meal can best enjoy the delicacies of a scrumptious woman. A man who cares how his food tastes also cares about the quality of his lovemaking.

It's no coincidence we use "appetite" and "hunger" for both sex and food. A man who gobbles down his food, drowning it in condiments, doesn't even know what he ate. He probably does the same thing in bed. This is definitely not the way to please a woman. A gourmet will view a woman as a meal to be savored course by course. In dining, as in love, he takes it slow, praises what he's getting, sharing the sensual experience with his woman.

The old adage, "The way to a man's heart is through his stomach," still applies, but it applies to women as well. When a woman cooks for a man or brings him little delicacies, it makes him feel that she cares about his well-being. Similarly, when a man wines and dines a lady, she usually feels more amenable toward him. It's obvious why sharing a meal is seen as the cornerstone of seduction.

The way a man eats tells a woman a lot about his

character, manners, and background. Behave well while eating, whether she cooks for you or you eat out. Once I went to dinner with what I thought was a perfectly charming man. The conversation was lively, his table manners flawless. The check came and he paid it, tipping generously. He then picked up his cloth napkin, blew his nose slightly, and threw it onto his plate. I was so embarrassed, I wanted to leave through the kitchen. This display told me that he had kept up a big front for much of our date, but it wasn't a natural part of his character. I was disappointed.

What follows is my essential collection of good manners and style—etiquette that's guaranteed to serve you well with the ladies, and in your social life generally.

Start by choosing a restaurant that pleases her. Feel her out; say, "I hope you like Italian food because I'd like to take you to my favorite Italian restaurant." This leaves her the opportunity to say, "I'd love to," or "I'm on a diet, I'd prefer something on the lighter side." Tell her how formal or casual the place is so she knows how to dress. The last thing you want when you fetch her at the door is for you to be wearing your best suit and her wearing jeans. If this happens, say the Italian place is too ordinary, and you know this funky little French restaurant down the street. Your enthusiasm will cover any miscommunication.

If you're habitually late, plan to be at her door fifteen minutes early, so that you can be your usual fifteen minutes late and still be on time. If you're the kind of guy who insists on punctuality and she's late, swallow it the first time, but let her know in a sensitive way that it doesn't thrill you when you have to wait. At least you're communicating. If she likes you, she'll try not to do it again.

Take her to a restaurant where you have already dined, so that you feel comfortable there and will be able to suggest some special dishes. It doesn't have to be expensive—choose whatever is most appropriate for her. If she's the type who drools over power, and you're a powerful kind of guy, definitely take her to the place where you're known and where you get first-rate service. If your budget is limited, and you're dining at the neighborhood Chinese restaurant, you can still act with perfect etiquette—in fact, you can have more fun in such places!

The first step is to call in advance for a reservation. If you're not led directly to your table when you arrive, you will probably find a reception area with chairs. Invite your date to sit down and order her a drink, if she likes. Always help a woman put on and take off her coat or wrap.

After you're called to your table by the maitre d', offer your date her choice of seats. If he doesn't help your date with her chair, then, of course, you should assist her. She might change her mind and wish to change seats. Let her. Don't make her feel she's not free to move around.

If the waiter doesn't hand a menu to her first, but leaves them on the table or gives them to you, give one to her first, then look at yours. (You may want to read one together.) If you know the restaurant and its specialties well, particularly the foreign or exotic dishes, suggest some choices to her. If both of you are unfamiliar with the menu, ask the waiter to recommend one of the specialties of the house. Listen to her suggestions—she may open you up to some new possibilities. Women like to see a man try different things. If she asks "Have you ever tried oysters?" and you say "Ugh, no, I couldn't!" she immediately knows more about you than you'd like. Take a deep breath and go for it. Try new foods with an open mind and open mouth. At least it might be an opportunity for laughter.

Traditionally, the man orders for the woman, but

today most waiters will ask the woman for her order. If you've already agreed on what you both want, it's fine (and sexy!) to take charge and do the ordering, but if you haven't decided, don't assume you know what she's hungry for. If she chooses an item that you can't afford, suggest a similar, less costly item. Does she really want a Crab Louis (at $22.00) when the shrimp cocktail (at $11.00) is just as appealing? She'll understand. Again, humor is the great antidote.

At an informal dinner, a light red wine such as a claret may be drunk from the beginning of the meal. The convention is to serve a well-chilled dry white wine with fish or poultry and a full-bodied red wine with red meats, duck, and game. All red wines are served at room temperature, but burgundies can be a degree or two warmer if the vintage is very good. The waiter should offer you the cork to sniff and inspect first, so you can check that the wine hasn't "turned" (is overly fermented), in which case the cork will have a vinegary smell and most likely a crumbling texture. This rarely happens with modern refrigeration, but if it does, by all means ask for another bottle. He will then pour a small amount into your glass. Swirl it, smell its aroma, and have a taste before nodding that he can serve your date. Or you could demonstrate you're a liberated man by allowing her the option of approving the wine!

White wine glasses should be picked up by the stem rather than the bowl, to keep them cool. Reds are served in wide goblets that can be cupped with the hand to keep the wine warm and fragrant. They need to "breathe"; after a red is opened, let it sit for a while before drinking it.

Champagne, above all other beverages, is that of the formal dinner party. If drunk along with other wines, it is served with appetizers or dessert, but when it is the only wine, it is served as soon as the first course has begun. An excellent vintage champagne should be packed in ice. When opening, wrap the bottle in a towel or napkin as protection in case the cork pops without warning.

Vermouth or some other aperitif is served before the meal, and liqueurs, cognac, or brandy with the coffee or dessert. Hard liquors are served only with particular foods, such as vodka with caviar, herring, or smoked fish, and whiskey with British biscuits, olives, cheeses, and cold cuts. Beer is considered a soft drink, for consumption at sporting events, hamburger or hot dog places, or at home and with friends. Water should always be requested.

When you are at an ethnic restaurant, treat yourself to their special beverage: ouzo at a Greek restaurant, sake or Japanese beer at a sushi bar, green tea at a Chinese restaurant. Wines are especially fine in French and Italian establishments. Have an imported beer when eating German, Swiss, Austrian, British, or Australian.

During the course of a formal meal—soup, appetizer, main course (entree), salad and cheese, dessert, and beverage—offer the woman first choice of whatever is served, including the bread and butter. Wait for her to begin before you start eating.

Always start by using the outermost utensils, to the side or above your dish. Some foods, like fish, should be eaten with two forks, one holding the fish in place while the other removes unwanted bones and debris. (I prefer to have the waiter debone the fish for me; it's less trouble.) Spaghetti can spoil a promising evening. Don't twirl it in a spoon—they don't in Italy. Take small amounts and use the plate to twirl it onto the fork. Parmesan cheese makes the strands less slippery—that's why it's used so much in Italy and Sicily!

If you order something daring and she orders something plain, offer her a taste of your meal. Cut a piece off and put it on her bread dish or another small plate; don't plop something in her mouth like she's a trained seal. That's annoying, even if we like a guy. If she's ordered something salivating and you've ordered something bland, don't keep eyeing her plate. It's nerve-racking.

If your meal comes and you're not pleased with it, you have every right to send it back no matter where you're dining. But be careful about your attitude. I assure you, the restaurant didn't serve you bad food or wine on purpose, and it certainly wasn't the waiter's fault. Your date will be watching every move and deciding whether she really wants you depending on your behavior in this situation.

Once you have put food in your mouth, chew it with your mouth closed and swallow it. This sounds obvious, but you'd be surprised how many men don't do this simple thing. Also, don't talk with your mouth full.

Don't spit out unwanted food or let it fall from your mouth onto the plate. Pits from fruits should be eased onto a spoon at your lips and conveyed to safety. For complicated items like fishbones, insert your finger and thumb and remove between compressed lips, or put your thumb underneath it and use the other four fingers to form a screen over it. Wipe your fingertips on a napkin.

If your date excuses herself from the table, make the gesture of standing while you pull the chair out for her. If she pushes the chair back herself, you should still make the gesture of standing when she leaves the table. When she returns, pull the chair out a bit for her to be seated. I don't mean stand at full attention as though your army drill sergeant just came into the room. It's not a complete action, it's just the motion of standing. You don't need to draw attention to yourself for every well-mannered gesture you make.

A lot of people get excited when they order dessert because it's so scrumptious. If you see her eyes light up when she's looking at the dessert menu, you might say, "Why don't you order something for me. The only thing I don't like is ———." In doing this, you're giving her some information about yourself and you're also giving her some power. That's fun for her.

If your date's purse, napkin, or anything else falls from the table, pick it up. Don't hesitate and bang heads with her as you both go down. Don't call for the waiter to fetch it. Be attentive.

Find a comfortable sitting distance from the table—not so close that your elbows will be in your plate, nor so far back that food will fall between your legs in transit to your mouth. Remember your body language, and sit straight but not stiffly. Don't look around the room at other women, and don't fumble, fiddle, or rock in your seat. If you need anything on the table, don't stretch your sleeve past your date's nose. If it's not within your reach, ask—it's an opportunity for a look, a smile.

When you're finished with your meal, place your knife and fork parallel to each other in the upper right portion of the plate. If you are still eating, your knife and fork should be placed at right angles to each other in the portion of the plate furthest from you. When using your napkin, blot or pat the lips. When you get up from the table, put the napkin on the right side of your plate, or, if the plates have been removed, in the center. Do not refold it or crumple it. Just lay it on the table in loose folds so that it doesn't spread out.

If toothpicks are on the table or counter, help yourself, but don't use them sitting at the table. Digging at food left in the crevices of the teeth is a less-than-appealing sight. Don't think that sucking on your teeth is a discreet alternative either!

To summon the waiter, catch his eye, then raise your hand slightly with a raised index finger. If you have to call, call quietly, or ask a waiter nearby, "Please call our waiter." Don't snap your fingers and yell, "Hey, waiter, come here!"

Have whatever money, in whatever form, the evening requires. After dinner, you might need a few small bills for the parking attendants. Always have extra cash in case of an emergency. Once, a date spilled burgundy on my white chiffon dress. He immediately placed sufficient cash on the table and we were out of there before it had a chance to dry and ruin the dress.

Now it's time to call for the check. This can be tricky. It's very impressive if a man is able to look at the check quickly and figure it out. If you spend a lot of time adding, reading, and rehashing, getting out reading glasses, calculators and pencils, she's going to get the idea that you're more conscientious about your money than her time. You should be able to tell in a flash if you've been given the wrong check or if they're off by a lot without losing the momentum of the evening. A quick mind is very sexy.

A 15-percent tip in any restaurant is standard; however, if the service was excellent, 20 percent may be in order. When you leave, tip the headwaiter in proportion to the service rendered. Tip generously but not lavishly.

OK, so the meal has passed without mishap. You fetch the car and pull up to where she is standing. Get out to open and close the car door for her; keep an umbrella in the car for this purpose in case it's raining. Never sit in the car, blow the horn, unlock the door, and wait for her to get in.

Perhaps she would like to go somewhere else for

an after-dinner drink (if she drinks), or somewhere different for dessert. But if it's already late and you must get up early the next day, then say to her *nicely*, "I could spend all night talking to you, but I've got to get up early in the morning. Is it all right with you if we call it an evening?" She will respect you for your honesty. Bon appetit!

4

· · · · · · · · · · · · · · · · · ·

Know
Her
Body
—and
Yours

Trifles make perfection,
and perfection is no trifle!
—MICHELANGELO

MALE AND FEMALE SEX ORGANS

The first point I have to make is that *your genitals are not dirty!* They're actually very beautiful and fascinating. The intrigue comes from their function, and the pleasure they can give to you and a woman is immeasurable.

Aristotle said, "You should know how to be your own doctor past thirty." If you know your own body well enough to take care of a small crisis, you'll save time and money by not running to a physician every time you sneeze. Also, if you're not sensitive to your own body, how do you expect to be sensitive to a woman's body which is far more complex? When you have a better understanding of the delicacy and softness of feminine tissue, you might pause and be more gentle when you enter your lover's vagina.

Our physical differences are obvious. Boys have a substantial amount of testosterone, the male sex hormone flowing through their bloodstream. Girls have estrogen, the female sex hormone clamoring through our sweet bodies. Yet in their development and basic structure, the male and female sexual organs are in many ways identical.

I was amazed to learn that in the early stages of fetal development, as the fetus grows, a penis develops in the male from the same tissue that develops into a clitoris in the female. Structures or tissues derived from the same tissue are called homologues. The penis is the homologue of the clitoris, the testicles are homologues of the ovaries; and the scrotum is the homologue of the labia majora (outer vaginal lips).

This information tells you that 95 percent of the human body is practically identical in structure in both male and female, except for the invisible Y chromosome. The male sex hormone is existent in extremely small amounts in every female, just as the he-man produces his supply of estrogen. It's our conditioning society that thrusts a football into little boys' hands while placing a doll into little girls' arms; these gender roles are not prescribed by a child's sex. It's pants for the XY and dresses for the XX.

HERS

When a woman spreads her legs wide, she exposes the most important part of the female external genitalia, the part that's shrouded in mystery—the vulva. Have you ever heard the phrase "mound of Venus"? It's a loose translation of the latin term *mons veneris*, which has been shortened by usage to *mons*, and is the area of fatty tissue that forms a little mound over the pubic bone. It's covered by skin and pubic hair. That's why when you gently tug at it, it awakens the underlying elements into sexual arousal (picking hairs and pulling would hurt, but taking several from the base and tugging lightly is sexy).

The labia majora extends from the mound of Venus tapering below the vaginal opening. This fold of skin involves nerve endings, oil and sweat glands, and fatty tissue. For protection to our sensitive area, pubic hair grows on the outer lips as they meet and cover the urinary and vaginal openings.

Because of the vast differences among females, especially in the genital area, a labia can have many folds or it can be smooth. One side can be smaller or larger than the other. As in a pair of natural breasts, each one differs in size and shape. The labia can look closed or open and vary tremendously in color during sexual arousal. Also, the inner lips (labia minora) can either fit inside the outer ones, or they can protrude. The appearance does not have anything to do with a woman's history of sexual activity or her ability to enjoy it. Some women are born with hanging lips and folds that have nothing to do with childbearing or sexual intercourse; others are born with smooth, matching lips.

The inner lips extend from directly above the clitoris to the vaginal opening. These matching folds of skin are hairless and devoid of fatty tissue. They also have more nerve endings than their outer sister, making them more sensitive. Again, it's not unusual for them to protrude. The color will vary from pink to purple to red to black. They are all normal and change during arousal.

The clitoris is located just below the top of where the lips meet. Push the little hood (prepuce) upward, if you want to take a good look. The clitoris is also covered by the labia and extends inside the body to the area of the pubic bone. Unlike the penis, it does not carry urine; its sole purpose is receiving pleasure and focusing that same sexual stimulation toward greater heights. (The clitoris, like your penis only shorter, is made of erectile tissue—it engorges with blood and is very responsive.) Slightly below the clitoris is the urinary opening (urethral meatus) which is exactly like the urinary opening in the man's penis. It is the site where urine exits from the female genitalia

The urethral meatus is the area where a woman sometimes ejaculates fluid if she has a certain kind of orgasm. The fluid is similar to your semen. However, it's not as thick and obviously carries no sperm. This fluid is sometimes tart and sometimes as sweet as nectar. It can also be either clear or milky, depending on the woman's health, time of her cycle, diet, and exercise—it all plays an important role in determining taste and appearance. Again, it varies from woman to woman as the taste and smell of semen varies from man to man.

Now you're headed for the "entrance" (introitus). The vagina, just below the urethral meatus, is the largest tube of the female genitalia—three to four inches long and flexible. When aroused, the vaginal wall produces a slippery liquid that helps your penis slide in smoothly. Next is the cervix (Latin for "neck"), which protrudes into the deepest part of the vagina and can often be felt during intercourse. The cervix is the bottom part of the uterus, which is a hollow organ about three inches long and two inches wide and shaped like an inverted pear. Attached to the uterus are the two fallopian tubes and two ovaries (each about the size of a grape). The ovaries produce eggs and sex hormones.

Basically this information is all you need to know for now, because this area is where you slide your pride. Women complain about men rubbing them raw during intercourse and not knowing how to touch their bodies. Maybe this will answer a lot of questions and explain how you could be accidentally hurting her. Multiply your genitalia sensitivity by ten and you'll have some idea of the sensitivity of her private parts!

YOURS

The penis is composed of three rods of erectile tissue encased in skin, which become hard and responsive when stimulated. An erection occurs when feelings of sexual arousal are processed in the brain and then relayed through the nervous system to the penis. It can also be caused by physical irritations such as tight pants or vibrations. The penis then swells and hardens because the muscle at the base tightens and closes the passageways that normally allow blood to escape the rods of erectile tissue. During the course of one night a man who is sleeping could have as many as five erections, each lasting approximately thirty minutes. This is true even of impotent men. Impotence is a dysfunction of the mind. The mind refuses to follow the body's command to produce an erection, but the penis can still produce semen and ejaculation.

The "average" length of a flaccid penis is four inches, but it may be as short as two inches or as long as seven. When erect, the average is about six inches, within a range of four to ten. Smaller organs actually increase more than proportionately when aroused; thus a four-inch flaccid penis will reach the same size as a flaccid six-incher when hard. The size of a man's penis is certainly not related to his body size. A boy's penis usually reaches its adult proportions around the age of seventeen.

When a man ejaculates, several powerful muscle contractions eject less than a tablespoon of semen. The sperm, carried by the semen, travel through the urethra (the hollow tube in the center of the penis, used also for urinating) and spurt out from the opening in the tip of the penis. Because the muscles that close the veins during erection also close the outlet from the bladder, a man cannot urinate when sexually aroused. I'm sure you know *that* feeling!

Your sperm is manufactured in your testicles and mixed with seminal fluid, which is a product of the prostate gland. The seminal fluids will provide your sperm with the energy it will need to swim the long distance up the female reproductive tract and fertilize her egg, perhaps days after ejaculation. (That's the reason why you must *always* know where a woman is in her menstrual cycle and use a condom—it's very important!)

Sperm comprises only two percent of semen. This fluid also contains thirty-two different chemicals, including vitamin C, vitamin B12, sulphur, zinc, and potassium. (Swallowing semen is healthy!) Right after ejaculation your semen gels and then liquefies again after about five minutes or so. This is designed to assist mobility of the sperm and is due to enzyme action.

After ejaculation, the erectile rods shrink and soften, and the veins open to drain the blood away. The penis then returns to its flaccid state. Some men are ready to have another erection right away, but most need to wait at least twenty minutes, known as a refractory period. This, however, depends on the age of the man and the strength of his sex drive.

The general consensus of women I interviewed is that the first three inches of a man's penis are the most significant, because the most sensitive and pleasurable part of a woman's anatomy is the entrance to her vagina. In the male anatomy, sensitivity is also near the top or head. Women like the top of the penis to tease and move gently in and out of their entrance, before engulfing the whole organ. A knowledgeable man uses his penis in the same manner he uses his tongue— getting a woman so turned on by this delicate action that she begs him to plunge deeper. She might grab his buttocks to show when and how she wants the rest of what he's got to give.

Every woman is built differently and will have her own viewpoint on penis size and shape. A woman's preference will be the penis that makes her feel comfortable, loved, excited, and gives her *satisfaction!* Physiologically, a vagina can receive pleasure from nearly any size penis. But psychologically, some women think an unusually well-endowed man is superior in bed. A large penis triggers a woman's fantasy.

Lucy, an eighteen-year-old curly strawberry blonde, prefers a large penis because she enjoys putting it between her breasts and armpits, and stroking her face and body with its thickness. She derives more pleasure from playing with it than from actual penetration. The visual alone sets Lucy on fire.

The irony is that in practice, it's often the less endowed men who give more pleasure. Many of the women I interviewed slept with men who thought their length and thickness enabled them to all but skip foreplay. This type of man is usually so wrapped up in the superiority of his size, he doesn't take the time or make the effort to properly lubricate the woman to receive his endowment. This is especially unpleasant if it happens to women who are young and sexually inexperienced.

Thirty-five-year-old Betsy said she believes a man with a smaller or average penis is more enthusiastic and passionate, and makes a tremendous effort to please. When Betsy met Buck, the first thing he said was, "I don't care what these other men are promising you, I'm prepared to give it to you!" She couldn't wait for the show to begin.

Buck was tall, with a great sense of humor, a delicious full mouth, and a quite average penis which he nevertheless knew how to use. Buck was aware that a woman can have multiple orgasms and he set out to give them to Betsy through oral sex, tongue baths, massage, and whatever else in his pleasure repertoire it took to please her. Foreplay was long and adventurous, and every time he made love to her it was like the first time. She confessed that when he called her on the phone, she would tingle just listening to his deep, sensual voice.

The message is you don't have to win the *Penthouse* prize for "Salami of the Year" to be a great lover. You've got endless options to get a lady lusting for you. You can change a woman's life by using your imagination and sensitivity to take her to greater heights of eroticism. Her sexual appetite will increase along with her satisfaction no matter what your penis size; she will never be able to get enough of your instrument if you know how to use it.

When in doubt, a good rule of thumb is to do to your woman what you would like her to do to you. Listen to her body language; communicate with her on all levels. Explore and find out those magical things that really turn her on. A good lover relishes his beloved as if she were his last supper! As Mae West observed, "It's not the men in my life, it's the life in my men!"

FOREPLAY

I call "foreplay" *anything* before the act of intercourse that gets you excited.

Because we women are different in so many ways, it takes us longer to get excited. A woman needs a lot of kissing, caressing, and words of endearment. Most women agree they can only orgasm either through manual or oral stimulation, but not through intercourse alone. It's up to you, fellas, especially in our suddenly monogamous society. So always remember: Don't rush! If you rush through the preliminaries, you will miss the woman altogether.

A woman is like a fine musical instrument. If you know how to play the instrument, you can make beautiful music. I don't expect you to be Fats Waller, flying on his piano the first time around, but by getting in touch with your own sensuality—seeing, hearing, smelling, touching, and tasting—you will be able to enjoy the exploration of bodily pleasures which is foreplay.

You can take your lover down an incredible journey of eroticism, adventure, chills, and thrills. But you must *prepare* for the journey if you want your sexual symphony to reach its highest crescendo—a simultaneous orgasm. All your body parts play an important role in this great symphony—tongue, fingers, hands, mouth, penis, testicles. You need strength, endurance, and dexterity. Your body needs to be healthy and in good working condition so you can control any sexual situation.

Be relaxed and enjoy yourself, and she will relax as well. My cousin Hannah, who's a top model in New York and very successful with men, said, "I must have a man who is relaxed and fun to be with. I certainly don't want him to look like he's been hanging in a closet. Too much twisted steel loses its sex appeal!" This is Hannah's favorite expression when describing an uptight, stiff looking man. So stop worrying and enjoy her as you would your favorite meal.

Each body part is an erogenous zone, so treat it accordingly. Take it portion by portion. Don't gobble it up like you haven't eaten for weeks. Rushing shows little confidence, it's not sexy, and she could freeze up entirely. Remember: To be the best takes time.

Soft, romantic music, candlelight and wine can be a good start, but you might also be sitting on a mountaintop in your car with the full moon making your skin shimmer with a silvery glow. Wherever you begin, make sure it's comfortable and private. You want no interruptions.

All right, let's get down. Begin by looking in the woman's eyes: Undress her with your eyes, sense her aura, smell her aroma, pay close attention to every move she makes. Talk to her in your most soothing, deepest tone of voice and reveal a little of your true feelings. That really turns a woman on.

And then . . . the kiss. As Marlowe's Doctor Faustus said, "Sweet Helen, make me immortal with a kiss! Her lips suck forth my soul; see where it flies!"

Women love to kiss. Kissing is the most important element in seduction. There is nothing more sensual and erotic to a woman than a man's lips draining her strength and setting her body on fire with his kiss. If you do it right, words, thoughts, and ideas will be erased from her mind. As your tongue explores her lubricated mouth in a ritualistic dance, she will fantasize about your adventurer finding its fearless way into her Pandora's box. The mouth is key. It's the soul of the loins, and it will be your barometer of how far to go.

So here are a few things you need to know about kissing. First, relax your jaw. Since the muscles of the lips are connected to the jaw, when you relax your jaw, the lips relax. The kiss must be tender, delicate, and with controlled passion. Kiss gently at first. Cushion your lips against your teeth. She must not feel your teeth, just your soft, gentle lips. When you kiss a woman with tension in your lips, she automatically assumes you won't be a good lover.

Don't stick your tongue in her mouth before your lips have had a chance to meet. That's like trying to penetrate while you're shaking hands and saying hello. It's offensive and you might scare her away. After she feels comfortable you can gently but firmly rub the tip of your tongue over the front and back of both rows of her teeth. (Some women may not like this particular exploration. Her reaction will let you know.) It's also very erotic to delicately suck on her lips.

If she gives you her tongue, that means she has accepted you, and her sexual temperature is rising. But stay with sensual, tender, and exploring kisses. While you're delicately exploring her lips and mouth with your tongue, keep it narrow and pointed, rather than broad and flat. Don't suffocate her by keeping your whole tongue deep in her throat. If her mouth opens more, slip your tongue in a little further with the same feeling as though you were entering her down below. Remember to tease, so withdraw slowly to see if she's with you. If she is, proceed rhythmically with bolder strokes as though you were in the middle of passionate intercourse. A few women have told me that they can orgasm if the right man knows how to kiss.

You need to treat kissing with the same attention as you would cunnilingus or intercourse. Because if certain women don't like the way you kiss, you're not going to get anything else. Period. When you know for sure she is with you, move on to kiss other areas of her face—her eyes, her nose and her ears, then down to her neck. Now comes the next crucial element—touch.

What you do with your hands is oh so important in arousing a woman. Did you know that women fantasize about a man's hands? How he will touch her, where he will touch her, when he will touch her—hands are a *big* issue with women. Your hands will tell her how skilled you are in the art of touch and how much you desire her. Passionate women will suck every finger of the hands of the man they choose to touch their body. A man's hands can make magic. The right touch can arouse a slumbering libido she never knew she had.

As the kissing goes well, fondle her through her clothes. This will tell you two things: one, the shape of her body, and two, whether or not you'll be able to proceed with the undressing. If she won't allow you to fondle her with her clothes on, I don't think it's your night. Reevaluate.

Undressing a woman is also an art. After she's allowed you to fondle her body through her clothes, after she's accepted your massaging her breast, it's time for serious stimulation. While you're kissing her lips and massaging one breast, you could begin to unbutton, unzip, or slip down the top of her garment with your sensitive, nimble fingers. It's a good rule to start at the top. As you're pulling her garment down, kiss all along the sensual areas as described in the following paragraphs.

The key to undressing is to take a lot of time with each item of clothing and as you remove each part of her clothing, make love to that part of her body. However, it is up to you whether you leave parts of her clothing on or disrobe her completely, as long as she likes it as well. Some men prefer a naked body, other men enjoy their woman wearing a few articles of clothing or lingerie. Just as certain women delight in leaving their stockings and garter belt on, others, who don't wear underwear, prefer you lifting their dress above their hips while making love. Different times and surroundings dictate different actions. Nothing is etched in stone!

Massage is a great prelude to lovemaking. It breaks the touching barrier, and relaxes the whole body and mind. In a matter of a few minutes you can soothe, energize, or arouse. You can warm her muscles, loosen tissue, and vanish away cramps and symptoms of fatigue. You're the musician, so learn to play her muscles, nerves, skin, and all her other erotic connections. It's the easiest way to relax a woman. It always works!

Give her a complete massage, if you have the skill and motivation. If you don't, begin with the lady on her stomach and massage the group of muscles in the back of the neck and shoulders, since this is where people hold the most tension. Place your fingertips on her shoulders and gently stroke around, across and up the neck, into the back of the head and all around the skull, then back down applying more pressure. Never let your fingers lose contact with her skin while rhythmically pumping the muscles. Return to the top of the spine and slide both thumbs down the sides of the spinal column. If she enjoys this, reverse the movement. Then gently with the heel of your hands use a zig-zag movement down the spine while blowing air on and kissing each vertebra.

For arms and wrists, squeeze and release, squeeze and release, all the way up to her shoulders. And for men that have foot fetishes, this is a perfect opportunity. Take her foot in your hands and hold it for a few seconds, letting your warmth and energy penetrate into her nerve endings, before you begin manipulating it. Feel the structure and massage the metatarsus (the five long bones of the foot). Make sure you massage all five. Then concentrate on the toes, giving each one a gentle tug. From toes follow with the instep, heel, ankle, calf, knee, thigh, and on up the body. To do this simple massage, the lady should be on her stomach first. When you've finished, ask her to please turn over on her back. (A professional masseur will always begin with the woman on her stomach.)

Once you're sure she's relaxed and she is on her back, let movements become caresses. Start caressing and softly kissing her neck, shoulders, lips, and face. You will begin to feel her warmth if she's responding. Pull her bra strap down and kiss that area with your mouth and tongue and then put the strap back up. This is teasing!

Lick and kiss the throat, murmuring compliments like, "Hmmm . . . you taste delicious. I love that perfume. I didn't know a woman's skin could feel so soft." Say the words that you feel in your heart. Express your true feelings about her, what you want to do to her and how you want to do it, sensually. What you *don't* want to be whispering in her ear is how much money you made last week or that you finally got that promotion. The only dialogue at this time is flattering and sexy talk, with your focus on her.

Everything is rhythmic. That's why I stress body movement. It's so important to be graceful when you're positioning her body at different stages of lovemaking. You must keep in mind the timing and rhythm of the moment. You don't want to be doing a rumba while she's waltzing, do you? Stay in tune with your musical instrument, your woman. Play her like Segovia stroked his classical guitar and her face will start to flush and her nipples protrude from her blouse.

Hold her hand and massage the palm while putting each finger in your mouth, one by one, sucking seductively and looking deep into her eyes. Let your tongue proceed up her arms and neck to her eagerly awaiting mouth. Kiss and gently bite her earlobes while breathing warmly into her ear.

With the tip of your tongue, gently trace the outline of her ear, every so often slightly inserting your tongue into the ear. Don't drown her hearing with a lot of tongue and saliva. It will take her out of the mood you've been creating. Whisper sensual and endearing secrets, and delicately insert your pointed tongue. She will be able to think only of your penis entering her vestibule.

You've had your drink and appetizers—now it's time for the next course! Hold her head back with your fingers and trace your tongue down her neck, planting tender, little kisses as you go. Put your fingers in her hair and gently tug on it. Most women really love you to put your fingers through their hair and smell it as you caress it. It's hot! It tells her how much you appreciate every part of her anatomy as you move on to her breasts. (Make certain she's not wearing a wig or extensions. You might ask softly if it's okay to massage her scalp.)

Women have realized, from time immemorial, that a heaving bosom naturally attracted men. Cleavage was and still is enough to send a man's member throbbing. Women know they have a powerful weapon.

That may explain why thousands of women seek surgical augmentation.

As you know, there are varying sizes of breasts, and they all deserve your undivided attention. You may ask yourself, "Should I make love any differently to a larger breast as opposed to a smaller one?" Yes! A large bosom usually evokes the child in you—there's more play, more toying around with it. And, you may tend to spend more time, because it provides a sense of comfort. But don't neglect the smaller ones. Give them all of your attention with more focus on the nipple, until you see the areola (the area surrounding the nipple) blossoming to its fullest.

Without breaking rhythm, continue with the impression of your soft, moist lips down her neck, creating a little suction with your lips and tongue as you slide in between her breasts. With the tips and pads of your fingers, tease around the breast. I know most guys are breast worshippers, but true "breast men" are more into shape than size. And worshipping a woman's breasts doesn't necessarily make her feel good. Touching the breast is an *art*—enjoying its response and watching it come alive is your *reward*.

Women agree that men often bite insensitively, suck too strongly, and grab too hard. Take one breast at a time and arouse her in separate stages. Continually tease! That sensual moment of your mouth to her breast should be relished, so take your time. Skip over the nipple until the last stage. It's key. Your fingers should feel like feathers, your mouth a caress. Vary your strokes—delicate to firm, delicate to firm.

Take both her breasts in both your hands, massaging gently while you take a nipple between your lips—licking, fluttering, sucking, alternating from one nipple to the other with the same fervor. Then roll your thumb and index finger on the nipple in the same man-

ner you would roll a grape without breaking its skin
—*gently*, yet stimulating. She's certain to feel your hot
persuasion and see admiration in your eyes at every
stage. Remember it should be like the first time you've
ever seen a breast and yet you know exactly what to
do, naturally!

Make her desire you just as you're desiring her.
Make her *suffer* by your slow, ever so slow, gentle
moves of touching, licking, wet lips, massaging, and
by making her wait, wait, *wait* until you're ready to
show her what you've got. She will just tremble with
excruciating passion and desire.

Because you're holding back, you are driving her
crazy. She loves it and she hates it. Good for you! She
loves the desire you're creating, but she hates you for
not giving her what she craves. At the same time, she
appreciates your control, your manliness, your confidence in making her squirm for your body. *That*, darling, is the *supreme* aphrodisiac!

A woman loves a man who knows what he's doing
and who's always in control. It allows her to surrender
to her own erotic notions. The message that you're
giving to her brain is, "I'm dying to send my explorer
into your innerspace, but I'm going to make love to
every part of your body until you beg for more."

Now that you've touched her breasts with your
fingers, cup them in your hands and play with her
nipples gently with your tongue. While your mouth
draws suction from one nipple, have your hand fondle
the other. Then change and give the other nipple your
undivided attention. She's your favorite dessert and
you're draining sweet nectar from her breast. (During
and before her menstrual cycle, her nipples may be
extra sensitive, so please take care at these times. She
will appreciate your knowledge and concern.) As you
feel her excitement build, alternate back and forth.

Hold them so she can see how firm you have made her. She'll die with desire.

Move down her stomach with the same attention and technique, massaging tenderly while nibbling on her belly button, and continue down the outsides of her thighs. With one hand, apply a little pressure just above the pubic hairs. That's a very sensitive area and extremely erotic to a woman. Even for a man to simply rest his hand on that area is warm and loving; she feels he's in tune with her womanhood. Also, you're directly over the G-spot. (More on that later.) Gently tug, but don't pull, on her pubic hairs—women love little tugs.

Keep one hand in the stomach area, while your other hand massages the outer leg and your tongue slides down the inner thighs to the knees, calves, ankles, and then her feet. Now your body is between her legs. As you massage the bottom of the foot with your fingertips, put each toe, one by one, in your mouth, sucking and circling your tongue around them. By this time, she'll feel like she's riding with you on a magic carpet, weaving in and out of the stars and circling the moon!

Always keep close contact with her body, whether it's your hands, your mouth, or your own skin. This contact makes her feel secure with you, and maintains the rhythm. When I say continue to touch, continue to lick, continue to massage, don't break your rhythm, because you are gradually pulling the arousal, the response, the passion from her body. From the point you begin your lovemaking, never break physical contact with the woman.

Lovemaking is not screwing! Lovemaking is exactly what it says—*making love*. It means loving what you're doing, loving the woman you're with, loving yourself, loving all the different feelings and sensations you're promoting in her and experiencing yourself. In lovemaking you draw feelings to the surface that were lying dormant. Or you bring out virgin feelings in both of you. The possibilities in the realm of lovemaking are simply mind-boggling. You can do no wrong when your body is in sensual accord with your lover. You're on the *same* note in the *same* song of the *same* musical score.

Sometimes it will be a faster rhythm, sometimes it will be very slow. Lovemaking has many peaks. Thelonious Monk and Joe Sample make love to their pianos, make them sing. Louis Armstrong and Miles Davis did the same with their trumpets. When Jimi Hendrix took his guitar in his mouth, it wasn't for show. It was because he *just couldn't get enough of it* with his hands and needed more direct contact. That's the feeling you want to go for—complete absorption in your lover.

Trace your tongue back up her legs to her inner thighs. Shift her legs up over your shoulders, her calves onto your back, and put your hands under her buttocks to steady her pelvis. Your thumbs should be free to deliberately tease her now, so gently press the tips of your thumbs against the area between her vagina and her anus. Slide the thumbs up to the inner lips. Now separate your thumbs and slide them outward, traversing the outer lips, then back up to the inner lips and so forth. Repeat this a few times.

With your tongue, begin making circling motions tracing the outer portion of the clitoris. Remember, her clitoris is like the head of your penis so you don't want to grab and pull. You want to tease her clitoris the way a woman would tease the frenulum of your penis (you know, the area that goes into a V, which is your most sensitive), so be extra, extra tender.

You're calling the shots, so stay confident. Choose the moment to intensify her thrill by slightly pulling back the little hood with your thumb from the top and quickly flicking your tongue across the exposed clitoris.

Remember it's sensitive, so take care to keep the touch light. Her legs will probably be squeezing your shoulders tightly. Since you're searching for her rhythm, pay attention to the way she squeezes her legs and the way she moves her body. At this point, if you're in synch with her rhythm, you can give her an orgasm with your tongue and the suction of your lips.

Gently cup your hands under her buttocks to secure your contact while your tongue is flicking in different directions across her clitoris. It will feel great to her if you can expertly massage her buttocks with the same rhythm that your tongue massages her clitoris. Feel how she responds.

If she doesn't like what you're doing, *stop*. If she's delirious with pleasure, continue with exactly what you've been doing. You're making her believe if she wasn't in love before, she's well on her way now! Don't change rhythms or positions. Lori says the biggest mistake her husband makes is changing positions. "Just when I'm getting ready to come, he moves or changes rhythms and all is lost. I get so frustrated because I'm almost there!"

Now go around the lips (labia) again with your tongue and slowly insert it into the entrance of her vagina. Put it in as deep as you can, then withdraw. Use a similar motion with your tongue as you would your penis. Tease her with it a little, then give her more, more, more until it's all in. Withdraw again and again, always teasing, always exploring.

She'll orgasm all night, if you have a slow hand and an easy touch and you delight in teasing. Would you like to know just how good you are if you can't tell by her secretions? Put your finger inside the vagina and feel for the contractions of her P.C. (pubococcygeus) muscles, also known as vaginal muscles. They're the ones that grab onto your penis and suck. If they are contracting around your finger and extremely wet, then you know she wants you. (A few women don't like digital stimulation of their vagina. It's probably because they've never been aroused sufficiently to make an erotic connection with their man.)

Try different combinations with your tongue—circular motions, quick flutters, long up and down licks, gentle little suctions, slight blowing or running your nose back and forth. Build her up to a more heightened sexual state. She must be thoroughly and completely aroused before you make way for your homecoming.

For a little variety, some women find spanking invigorating, but it should never be done to hurt. In your fantasy playing, at the appropriate time, put your lover over your knees or lap, and with your hand semi-cupped or with the tips of your fingers, firmly tap her buttocks as you speak. I say firmly, because each tap should have a little stinging effect. It's the position and the sound that's effective—if it's too light, it doesn't work, but if it's too hard, it's not at all sexy, and if you actually hurt her she'll be mad.

With each little tap, tell her things she's done to displease you until she says she's sorry and she won't do it again. I'm sure you can think of a few things even if she's perfect! The idea is to give her pleasure, nothing but pleasure. Lisanne, a music teacher from New Jersey, told me she dated a pianist once. She'll never forget how one day he threw her over his knee and proceeded to spank her with one hand while he massaged her clitoris with the other. She said, "I felt like he was playing Chopin on *my* piano!"

When you're kissing or stroking her buttocks, give little nibbles and bites, or alternate between gentle and firm squeezes as you lick in between the crack, which is a real turn-on for most. If your lady likes this, proceed with gentle probing and well-lubricated fingers, then perhaps a little deeper if she's willing. You should gently rub her clitoris at the same time. It will certainly give her optimum pleasure! (Remember: Some women do, some don't.)

CUNNILINGUS

"To the left, nooooo, to the right, higher, further to the right, hummmmmm . . . hold it, yes, ohhh W-A-R-D . . . Ward, yes, yes, that's it, right there, oh yesssssss! Thank you. That was wonderful, darling, thank you!" said a grateful Lucille after husband, Ward, had given her the usual. This is called verbal communication. An experience not many people can share.

Cunnilingus is much, much more dependent on your technique and expertise than intercourse. During cunnilingus, a woman's body sensations are quite different than the ones she experiences with your penis inside her vagina—even though they're both nirvana. It's not possible to excel in this art without knowing your lady's intimate anatomy; ergo, the lesson preceding.

Your mouth is a highly mobile organ set in a highly mobile head and therefore provides great sensitivity by the touch of the tongue. It is also vastly superior to your penis. Why? Because if she finds it difficult to orgasm with "Mr. Happy" or if "Mr. Happy" is tired, you will still be a success! A woman can enjoy a series of orgasms of varying intensities before she's completely content.

Your tongue and mouth are very versatile. They can suckle, moisten if necessary, and use varied caresses. That pointed instrument can tickle, tease, and write the alphabet on her clitoris. It's totally at your command. If you're an artist with your mouth, you can be Picasso with a mere stroke of the tongue and your woman will probably lubricate in ten to thirty seconds after you've applied your genius.

Celia had her own Picasso: "The most erotic intoxication I have ever experienced came from a man named Gus. During foreplay, Gus pressed his lips against my pubis, then expertly traced his tongue around the crevice. In my delirium, I felt his instrument playing over my clitoris with agility. He had such control. It seemed to be at his command. I mumbled something slightly between a gasp and plea and shifted my body forward. I began to shiver as Gus applied his tongue more feverishly to my clitoris, up and down my cleft, then inside searching farther and farther. I threw my head back, eyes closed, holding tightly onto the sofa where we lay. I noticed every so often he would glance up at my face as if my expressions gave him the freedom to explore.

"Gus was a new experience for me. He soon applied his mouth more firmly against my hood and folds while proceeding to compress his lips onto my clitoris, and began a vigorous suction. I was trembling, my thighs pressed tighter against his cheeks as my entire body contracted. Gus continued the same suction as I approached orgasm. I held his head firmly against my womanhood. He quickly slipped his hands under the cheeks of my buttocks. I pressed him even closer. 'That's it; that's heavenly!' My thighs became spasmodic, quivering to a different tempo than the rest of my body. Suddenly, a warm flow of secretions slipped into Gus's mouth."

To be able to do the "right thing," your attitude should be that your woman's vagina is another mouth, which it is! Most probably, you'll need to strengthen your tongue muscles. So a good beginning is to place a grape (the big, green variety) in your mouth, keeping it between your teeth and your tongue. With your tongue, carefully rotate the grape without breaking the skin. Enjoy the erotic sensations of playing with it. Use circular motions, up and down and sideways. Knead it carefully with your lips and tongue. Also, write out the alphabet on it. All this practice will prepare you for the real thing—your woman.

After you become proficient and comfortable with a large, green grape, graduate to the smaller, more delicate, purple variety. Work up to the same rhythms and speed as the grape plays in your mouth. But remember, the key is not to break the grape. Practice until your tongue flutters and rolls it effortlessly. You absolutely must have a grasp on the grape!

Now, for the *cherry!* Maraschino cherry, that is. This is for real Olympians. Take a stemmed cherry from the jar, put it in your mouth, and use your tongue to tie a knot out of the stem. Don't despair if you can't do it. It's very difficult, and I've only seen it done a few times.

Poor tongue technique could cause the following to happen: Jenny, twenty-nine, an English professional woman, said her husband "sits me on his face and turns on the vacuum cleaner. It's awful—he doesn't seem to realize the pain he's provoking. I must say, it's terribly annoying, but I just don't have the heart to tell him he's been doing it wrong for years. He thinks he's great!"

To avoid being like Jenny's husband, don't bite it or suck as though your mouth were a vacuum cleaner with teeth, or nibble away like a chipmunk or peck at it like Woody Woodpecker. I don't know where men got this idea, but I assure you it wasn't from women!

Many men have never experienced giving cunnilingus, while others tried once and met with disaster. Either the woman refused or she had an unpleasant disposition. Whatever the dilemma, just know that cunnilingus should be explored only with a woman you know quite well and who is meticulous with her hygiene. It's not for strangers!

To insure cleanliness the two lovers should bathe or shower together. Bathing together is both intimate and fun. You could wash her, she could wash you. I know a man who gives his wife a douche as a method of foreplay. They both enjoy the stimulation.

Some lovers play fun games with each other's bodies. If your woman requests you give her oral sex, but you find the idea distasteful, play some games to make it more enjoyable: In the summer buy several flavors of ice cream and distribute three scoops onto her body—two scoops for the nipples and one, your favorite flavor, on the valley below. If it's winter, use whipped cream, honey, chocolate, butterscotch, or whatever you both prefer. Try a little Rachel Perry lip lover—it comes in many flavors. I'm sure you'll find one you like. Be inventive!

Be smart! Practice and listen to your woman's body language, her moans and groans. Be in tune with the unspoken. If you're lucky enough to be with a woman who communicates with you verbally, wow! You're on the money and well on your way to becoming an incredible, artful lover. Not only will you know how to pay attention to her instrument, you will also know how to touch it to drive her wild with delirious desire.

Mary Ann, an insurance underwriter from Indiana, offered another viewpoint: "It certainly helps when my man presses with one hand on my pubis. That puts more pressure on the genitals and pushes the clitoris down close to the opening of the vagina. In a teasing sort of titillation, he runs his tongue gently around and over my clitoris which is fine to begin with, but the more excited I become and the closer to orgasm I get, the more force I need. At that point, I push his head down harder and lift my hips up higher to make the pressure greater. When he takes my clitoris between his lips and sucks on it, it feels as if some powerful rhythm is rendering me helpless.

"Also, I can get a tremendous feeling when he moves his head rapidly back and forth or sideways, always keeping his lips on my clitoris. I think each time I have this experience, I desire it a little differently. Sometimes I want my man to run his tongue along the labia and put it in my vagina, while at other times I want him just to stay on the clitoris. I prefer when he changes rhythms. Variation is the spice of life.

"Sometimes I want to scream 'faster, faster!,' while on other occasions I like the lazy, slow motion and gentle feeling of his tongue barely touching the clitoris. Other times, I want him to put his finger inside my vagina, press the upper part and hold it there while he is performing cunnilingus. In certain positions, I feel the pressure of his chin against the outside of my vagina and labia and that adds immensely to my pleasure."

There are various ways to give this pleasure: with the woman on all fours and you in back; with her lying down and you between her legs; with her standing and you kneeling in front; with her bent over a car or desk and you in back; with her legs spread over your face as you're lying down; with her sitting on a countertop and you in front. If you're a large man and she's a tiny woman, you could lift her over your head while holding her legs apart and have dessert. I'm sure you can invent a hundred ways if you concentrate!

"Two years ago I met an unmarried, trained nurse named Julie ten years younger than I," reveals Jessica, a gynecologist in Los Angeles. "She was an experienced homosexual, who had never had a man. She took the initiative in mutual mouth relations. Julie preferred that and now I prefer it. More often than not, we did sixty-nine. But sometimes we would take turns.

"Our affair lasted for five months. Julie began by using her insatiable mouth and I was extremely hot most of the time. My husband used his mouth, too. Actually, it was my introduction to marriage and I loathed it. He didn't know the first thing about cunnilingus and I didn't know how to teach him. It was different with Julie. She taught me everything, but then, that's all she ever did!"

In another story I was told, a perfectly innocent girl was set up by a not so innocent girl. Jilly was invited to spend the weekend with Meg, a married friend whose husband was in Asia on business. She accepted. Meg was out to impress Jilly with her specialty—Italian cooking—and she succeeded. She also succeeded in relaxing Jilly with a smooth-tasting red wine. In fact Jilly drank more wine than she could handle, which put her in a carefree, funny mood. They started having a tickling match and somehow ended in the bedroom.

During the night, Jilly was awakened by soft kisses and caresses at her feet, then knees and thighs and she gradually felt her nightgown slide up. Meg then proceeded to separate Jilly's thighs and began kissing her genitals. She rolled on top of Jilly and began performing a tantalizing suction on her clitoris. At the same time Meg placed herself in the sixty-nine position, burying her genitals against Jilly's face. After a while, Jilly herself became so passionate she was delirious and couldn't resist Meg's artful and manipulative advances and soon fell limp in orgasm.

Beware: A common mistake many men make is losing the woman's clitoris during cunnilingus. It just disappears, so he thinks! If this occurs, gently massage your woman's stomach pressing your palm downward toward the vagina and the clitoris will reappear. You see, retraction of the clitoris at this heightened state is quite normal. And if you fail to continue stimulating the clitoral shaft, she will fail to orgasm. Don't stop because you can't feel it. She's in the process and to stop will be bad news for both of you! She will end up frustrated, unable to have an orgasm and you will go into her "Book of Stamps."

A few more common mistakes are diving for the clitoris too soon, before the proper amount of teasing of the "perfume garden." Remember to take your time. And using the same pattern on the same spot is boring and unimaginative; be creative. Don't assume she's finished after just one orgasm—most can have and want more.

A word to the wise: If you know a certain manipulation drives your woman up a wall with excitement—then bypass it and come back at a later time. It'll drive her crazy.

The clitoris is the most sensitive area of a woman's body. The size varies from woman to woman. Some are so small they are difficult to find, while others are large enough to protrude. How a woman enjoys sex has absolutely nothing to do with the size of her clitoris, any more than the size of your penis determines your sexual enjoyment. Again, it's not the grandeur of your gifts—it's the skill of sharing them!

INTERCOURSE

It ain't over 'til it's over!
—YOGI BERRA

When it comes to intercourse, most women are pretty simple. They don't care much for acrobatics, but rather "loving" intercourse—a union of body and mind. Before a woman reaches twenty-five, she's been through lovers who either stand her on her head or maneuver her spine into a backbend. For your information, guys, getting rug burns, a sprained back, a sore neck, or body bruises is not a woman's idea of a good time. Trying out for the circus is one thing; lovemaking is definitely another.

The skillful lover is both masculine *and* feminine. He knows how to elicit the fires of passion and to fulfill his woman's need for tenderness. He can bring out both the animal and the angel in his beloved. And he is master every step of the way, from slow, smoldering passion to final erupting abandon. It all comes down to being considerate of the woman and her needs at all times.

There's plenty for you to do in lovemaking without going out on a limb. That doesn't mean forfeiting a rich adventure. It means being imaginative and smart. When Marsha, a young accountant, was dating Chuck she related this story: "He asked me to go for a run on the beach, early one Sunday morning. We ran for quite a while, before I told Chuck I wanted to go back. He said we couldn't, because the tide had come in and the only way back was over the mountain. 'Over the mountain?' I gasped, looking up terrified. He motioned me to follow behind him.

"Battered and bleeding, I reached the top only to have Chuck fly at me like an eagle in an undulating, sexual frenzy. He undressed my tattered body and licked my nakedness from head to foot like a postage stamp. He threw this leg over that leg, this arm over that arm. I felt like a trained seal. The ten-mile hike back was not my idea of fun, either. The next adventure had me on a sail boat, which he couldn't sail—try having intercourse while swinging from the mast. Pasadena on Chuckie!"

Basically, the classic positions always work. In the sixties and seventies the clitoris was the focus of attention, stimulated by oral or manual means. This still has its place. However, in the nineties, we're back to the basic missionary approach, because coital orgasm can pleasure both mates simultaneously. But the only way to achieve this is to establish a common rhythm by following each other's instincts—doing the same thing at the same time, which provides greater pleasure for both lovers and allows the man to shine. To the woman he's in control because his manly self is spread out completely over her. She, on the other hand, is in the most extremely vulnerable position.

THE MISSIONARY POSITION

I feel the most important position is the missionary position simply because you're more likely to experience simultaneous orgasm. In this arrangement, the woman lies flat on her back, legs apart. The man stretches out on top of her with his weight supported by his arms and knees. It's almost like doing a push-up on top of her body. But be careful not to let all of your body weight collapse onto the woman. I'm sure you don't realize how heavy a manly body can be, and you certainly don't want to smother the poor woman underneath you. If you're not in shape, or you're tired from a hard day at work, it's OK to fall onto the side of her body without breaking rhythm in your love-making. Or if you're a tiny person and she's a big person, maybe she won't mind your body weight.

While in this position, the timing is a slow and gradual buildup. The idea is not for the woman to be passive and wait for you to penetrate, or for you to remain still and expect her to push into you, but rather to develop a gentle rhythm where both bodies work equally toward an imaginary center. (Pretend a furry ball or a pillow is between the two of you, and you're both trying not to let it slip or fall from that center.)

At first, both of you create a gentle, soft pulse which builds until you both explode at the same time. You are attentive to your own and her movements. Just like rafting down a river, you go slower or faster depending on the course. If you feel the woman is accelerating, adjust your pace to fit hers. If she slows down, she's probably not ready, so you slow down, too.

The key is unison: If she slows, you slow, if she speeds, you speed. If she starts bucking, ride it out. Don't freeze, definitely don't stop, and don't get scared, because she may already be in a series of linked orgasms and one of yours will absolutely coincide. However, if you orgasm first it's all over. The goal is to dance the sexual dance as if two were one. Stopping before her crucial moment by your premature orgasm or your hesitation will make her feel slighted or rejected or frustrated.

Remember, through orgasm she has opened herself. It's a vulnerable time, and she may be afraid to show her feelings if you appear unappreciative. So this would be a good moment for you to tell her how significant and important her orgasm is to both of you.

The specter of jealousy begins here. You may like to *think* you're the doer, but ideally, a natural rhythm links each of you, sometimes generated through your initiative, sometimes through hers. Don't misinterpret her aggression. It doesn't necessarily mean that she's jaded from having been with someone else. It just means she has picked up the natural flow of your lovemaking. Each individual is different and can create a unique, unexpected movement. It's intuitive, not learned. So accept her initiative. Don't read negativity into a positive situation. She's just feeling free and hot.

There are any number of variations of the missionary and I'm sure you will create your own. Her legs can rest on your shoulders or around your waist. You can put a pillow under her buttocks for deeper penetration. A pillow is always fun and useful. Experiment!

REVERSE MISSIONARY POSITION

The man lies on the bottom with the woman on top, her legs straddling his or extended directly on top of his. Sometimes a woman finds this position more orgasmic; she's able to guide and control your penis better with her pelvic muscles. And some women find it more comfortable, especially when they're making love to a man who is a bit overweight. But you mustn't forget that even when you are underneath the woman, you still have to work your buttock muscles in rhythm with hers.

ROLL-OVER POSITION

If the two lovers are in synch, it is customary to hold on to one another and roll over, landing in another position to continue your thrust. Do this only if you both have flexible bodies and fit well together. If not, your penis could fall out—a strange feeling—or you could possibly hurt yourselves.

ORIENTAL POSITION

You're on the bottom, she's on top with her legs drawn up close to her chest squatting over you. A woman with strong, flexible legs is able to lower and raise her body allowing your penis to go in and out. She can vary this by lowering her squat so that her legs rest on the bed, knees bent alongside of your torso. From here she can lean forward (chest-to-chest) or backward (bracing her hands on the bed or on your thighs).

CHAIR POSITION

While you sit in a chair, the woman sits on top of you. This is another position women find erotic. Again she's able to control her orgasm by controlling the amount of your penis she wants to allow inside her vagina.

DOGGY POSITION

This is a favorite with many women. She leans to all fours while you penetrate her vagina from the back, holding her hips tightly against your groin. It's a virile thing! Some women say they get a greater depth of penetration and can only orgasm in this position, while others cannot. This approach can be altered by lifting her up so that both of you are on your knees, her back to your torso. You can kiss her turned face, and massage her breasts and clitoris while you are simultaneously penetrating her vagina from the back.

POSTERIOR SLIDE-IN POSITION

Speaking of the back, the woman can lie on her stomach while you approach her vagina from behind, laying your chest on her back. She can enjoy the weight of your pelvis hitting her buttocks and the length of your penis traveling between her legs arriving at her vagina. During this adventure, you can put one hand under her pelvis and feel your penis hitting the palm of your hand through her body, a turn-on for both of you.

FACE-TO-FACE POSITION

If your woman is sitting on a sofa (or anywhere for that matter), separate her legs, get on your knees in front of her, and with one fluid motion, bury your erect shaft into her vagina and pull her torso close to yours. Now you're face to face.

YOGI POSITION

Both lovers sit on the floor facing each other. The woman sits on your crossed legs and inserts your penis inside her vagina while she crosses her legs behind your back. You need to be extremely flexible for this one.

CUDDLE POSITION

With both lovers on their sides (the man's front to the woman's back) the man slips his penis into her vagina from the back. The advantage is the snug fit, as well as the ability to massage the woman's breast and clitoris and hug her from behind. It's both cozy and comfortable.

WORKERS' POSITION

A slight variation of the cuddle. The woman rolls onto her back while you stay on your side. She lifts her leg closest to you and places it over your pelvis to give your penis access to her vagina. For comfort's sake, insert your top leg between her legs. From this position you can easily suck on her breast closest to you. This arrangement is commonly used by working couples who are exhausted at the end of a day but refuse to forfeit their sex time together.

As long as the position is comfortable, you can invent your own. It is essential to realize that positions are relative to the two lovers involved; the way the bodies fit will instinctively determine the use of positions.

This is a good time to explain the right way to penetrate. After all the foreplay, take your erection in your hand and swirl it around the outer and inner lips of her vagina, teasing slowly before you decide to insert the tip of the head. This is an exhilarating moment for a woman—the sensation when the penis first enters the lips is something a man can never know. So treat this moment with respect, and give your woman time to fully bathe in this special ecstasy.

Now ease your penis in slowly, but only give her a half inch at a time. Remember the teasing. This is the point where a woman feels the most pleasure from your member because it's touching her clitoris. The widest part of your penis is the head, therefore the in and out motion on its passage by the clitoris pleasures a woman the most. As it goes in, it turns upward, when pulling out, it feels like a ridge. On both accounts, you activate the clitoris. And if you go in and up at an angle, you'll also be touching her G-Spot—these are her two serious pleasure zones. Massaging her clitoris with your fingers is not necessary, but if you feel she could be more aroused, then by all means, do so.

After you've worked it in to almost the full length, gently withdraw. Then slide in and out again and again. The key is to create a honey-glazed torture. I know it's difficult, but, as Seneca said, "It's a rough road that leads to the heights of greatness!" And you're only as great as the woman you made love to says you are.

You want her to continue begging throughout the entire pursuit. Stay in control, be the guiding force. Her voice should be reaching high soprano by now and she will probably be demanding all you've got. But *never* give your entire length *until* her orgasm. Only then give it up!

When the party noise is a memory, and you both lie completely satisfied in the silence, *never* turn away from your lover. It doesn't matter if you're married, it doesn't matter if you have intercourse five times a day—in a woman's mind, there is no excuse for her man to fall asleep, get out of bed, or leave her until he has devoted the proper time to the resolution stage of making love.

The "afterplay" is just as important to a woman as your romantic advances are at the beginning of the dance. If you're really tired, just hold her in your arms and let her head rest quietly on your chest. If you have energy left, stroke her hair or face, tell her how wonderful she makes you feel, how big you can get because of her, how much you care.

If you love her, always tell her so. Whatever you say during this time must be felt from the heart. *You must mean every word you say, or say nothing.* This is her most vulnerable time. She needs to know that she's with a real man. And a real man doesn't take just any woman, either. He only goes after the best, because he's the best. And he will always tell the truth. It's the code of honor he lives by. That's why he deserves her admiration and respect—he's earned it.

WHAM! BAM! THANK YOU MA'AM!

Many men mistakenly believe that great sex is pounding a woman's vagina fast, furious, and repetitively.

Martha, a busty blonde from Missouri, confided, "A man I'd been dating for a while just pounded the living daylights out of me. Because I wasn't lubricated it hurt like hell and I got vaginitis from the considerable friction." I asked, "Didn't you tell him during the love-making that he was killing you?" "No," she answered. "I thought he would be able to tell from the pain showing on my face."

According to Alexia, a Raquel Welch look-alike from Chicago, "All men want to do is play Cowboys and Indians and go *bang, bang, bang!* How do they expect us to have an orgasm with all that banging? I have to dig my fingernails into my boyfriend's tight buns to slow him down. He stops for a few seconds, then, just when I feel it coming on, he starts that vigorous pumping again. I get a headache instead of an orgasm. For his next birthday, I think I'll buy him a blow-up doll so he can bang away until she pops!"

There are times when banging, pounding, and hammering can be terrific, but *not* unless she says so. If she's not telling you this is what she wants, the chances are she's not enjoying it. Don't be misled by the noise she might be making—you'd be making it, too, if you were the one being drilled.

It won't be the Fourth of July every time you make love. There will be certainly times that Superman will burst out of Clark Kent, but there will also be times when no matter what you do, you cannot bring a woman to orgasm. It takes two to tango, and without her desire, there's no guarantee. Maybe the next time she will be more receptive and willing. The answer doesn't lie in pounding her more—it lies in finding the special key that unlocks her mind and body. You won't find that key in the midst of gymnastics, or by humping and thumping her.

If you've exhausted your knowledge and magic tricks, maybe it's time to sit her down and have a little heart-to-heart talk. It's quite possible she's not telling you something that's vitally important to your love-making. Nothing can take the place of good communication and that's a fact! Be gentle, be patient. She'll eventually open up.

The opposite could occur, though, and the woman—after several orgasms—might insist on your pounding away when you're having a difficult time sustaining an erection, not to mention the twinges of pain as the sensitive shaft is rubbed raw. Stop hurting yourself! You're not competing in the Olympics. Let her know you're uncomfortable and I'm sure she'll understand. It's not about how many orgasms you can produce—it's an exchange of pleasure.

The sensation men and women feel after orgasm is very similar. When you have stimulated her to climax, the clitoris is at its height of sensitivity, and continuing to touch and massage it will not increase her pleasure. After you know she's climaxed, stop and allow her to enjoy the sensation. That exciting moment feels exactly the same for both male and female. So remember: When she hollers, let her go.

ORGASM AND THE G-SPOT

But the hour of vengeance falls, and I love you.
Body of skin, of moss, of eager and firm milk!
Oh the goblets of the breast! Oh the eyes of absence!
Oh the rose of the pubis!

—PABLO NERUDA

Have you ever been walking down the street and heard some Neanderthal yell, "You know what you need, lady?" The lady continues walking and ignores him. "What you need is a *good fuck!*" Well, gents, the gorilla is wrong—dead wrong! What the lady really needs is an *orgasm*. Like most women, she's probably had too many "fucks," and not one orgasm she didn't give herself. It's hard to believe, but it's true.

One of the most impressive movies I've ever seen is *Coming Home*, especially the scene where Jon Voight makes sensual love to Jane Fonda. Despite being a paraplegic, he was still the lover all women dream about—genuine, sensitive, knowing. His main focus was to give her pleasure and satisfaction. He couldn't do a particular act, so he did another. From Fonda's expression and reaction, one can see that Voight gave her an orgasm—something her husband never did. She expressed herself with gallons of joyful tears from years of suppressed release.

Do you want that special woman's hands all over you? Do you want her thinking about you every minute of every day? Do you want her to shiver at the mere thought of you? I should think any man would be delighted to have that certain woman think these things about him. Well, when you learn to give her orgasms, she'll be yours every time.

Now that you've read about the physical nature of womanhood and the techniques you should use to enjoy it, you should understand how to give a receptive woman an orgasm. I'm sure you would never want to get stimulated and then not get the chance to ejaculate. It's the same with a woman. You get her excited, you come, she doesn't—*bummer!* If this happens over and over, I'm sure I don't know why she would want to make love to you again. Life is frustrating enough; we don't need any added anxiety. We want release, relief, and ecstasy. The climax of sexual excitement and re-lease of massive energy is tremendously satisfying to all. So show her the way!

Unlike men, women can orgasm in several differ-ent ways, via clitoral, vaginal, or G-Spot stimulation. It's been proven that some women can orgasm by mere visualization. It sounds a bit farfetched, but it's true. And each kind brings on a different sensation. The women I interviewed concur that the most fulfilling orgasm is with a man's penis inside her vagina because it's emotionally more satisfying. Unfortunately, only 25 percent of the women I interviewed have experi-enced an orgasm from intercourse. Men, you need to do something about those numbers, pronto! A great many women orgasm through clitoral stimulation be-fore and during intercourse, which they say is more intense physically. But for us to receive any type of orgasm, we must surrender our bodies and our minds to your kind and skillful hands. Attitude is key, which is one of the reasons it's so important for you to re-assure and relax us.

There are women who can orgasm from deep kiss-ing, imagery, or by having a man suck their nipples. But these are highly erotic beings; everything they feel is amplified. It has something to do with their physical makeup and probably their mental and emotional makeup as well.

Most women, however, have a specific sexual po-sition in which they find it easiest to orgasm. Marissa, a thirty-three-year-old secretary, can only orgasm in the classic missionary position. She says she can control her muscles better when the man is on top rather than underneath. Lynn, twenty-eight, can only orgasm when she's on top. She becomes more aroused when she feels her breasts jiggling. Tammy, twenty-two, has found a way to orgasm only on her side with her man entering from behind. Christy, forty, said, "The only way I can orgasm is in the doggy position. I don't feel as guilty and I can lose myself in the eroticism." Lena, fifty, thinks they're all orgasmic.

There are certain women who will show you a few tricks of the trade. They know their bodies and they know yours. In any position they can manipulate their vagina to bring on complete satisfaction. You'll know when you're giving her this magic, because you'll see a complete metamorphosis. As a woman orgasms, her perineal muscles—the ones between the anus and the vagina—contract rhythmically. These reflexes resemble those that cause ejaculation in the male. The involuntary nature of these impulses is another reason you need to relax the woman through foreplay. Her body muscles contract, her eyes dilate, her breathing and the color of her skin change. Her uterus produces a suction effect that acts as a vacuum to suck up your sperm. Even if you don't ejaculate, you'll feel her muscles contracting around the stiffness of your penis.

At this time, a woman undergoes such a powerful and intense joy, don't be surprised if she bursts out in tears or laughs or both. She's having an out-of-body experience. There may be a certain sadness she will feel when it's over. It's heartfelt. Maybe it's an awareness of her own mortality. Whatever it is, be flattered that you have given her this high. Just hold her close in your arms, kiss her tenderly, whisper sweet nothings in her ear—and wait from ten to thirty seconds before you take her again! (Some women require a bit longer.)

Women, unlike men, can orgasm again and again

and again. There are four stages a woman reaches during sexual activity that Masters and Johnson called excitement, plateau, orgasm, and resolution.

Excitement develops during foreplay. When a woman gets excited, her vagina lubricates because her blood supply rushes to that area and causes engorgement of the surrounding tissue. When a man gets excited his penis becomes engorged with blood, producing erection.

Plateau is an advanced stage of excitement. Certain tissues in the vaginal wall swell, reducing the size of the opening. This allows the woman to grip your penis with her vaginal muscles. Her clitoris grows larger and becomes erect, then possibly retracts. In men, the testicles grow larger and are pulled upward, becoming compact. All your muscles increase their tension.

Orgasm is the muscular, rhythmic contraction of the vagina, at intervals of about four-fifths of a second. Then they become longer and intensify. There are major and minor orgasms. A major consists of about twelve contractions; a minor from three to five. The body undergoes physiological change: The pulse increases, the blood pressure rises, muscles spasm throughout the body, skin changes color, and breathing hastens. She may look flushed all over. However, at certain times an orgasm can be quiet and the only changes are the ones within, especially if she experiences many smaller ones and often.

Resolution is a stage of descent. If she's had one moderate orgasm, then the resolution will not be very long. If it was big or she had a few, it will take longer. But if she has not had one, it can last a long time. You know how you've felt on those occasions when your penis was erect for quite a while, but you didn't ejaculate? Same thing.

For multiple orgasms you need to keep her body at the plateau stage. If you wait too long and she cools off, you'll need to work twice as hard to make it happen again. In fact, ten to thirty seconds is about the right amount of time from orgasm to orgasm. Waiting beyond ten minutes may drop her into the resolution stage and that's not where you want her to be.

You know how sensitive you are just after ejaculation? Well, women are equally as sensitive, if not more so. To pump away during this highly escalated period of arousal might irritate rather than stimulate. Continuous delicate oral or manual stimulation would be the ticket, or you may want to rest inside her before you begin again—that's nice too. Basically, you want to gently keep your woman stimulated.

I must warn you that a certain percentage of women may never orgasm. The reason may be something deeply embedded in her subconscious. Perhaps she was molested as a child; maybe she feels guilt from a severe religious upbringing; maybe her father left home when she was a little girl; maybe she was raped as a teenager. Some women are not physically able to achieve vaginal orgasm and have had none of the above emotional traumas. They still enjoy sex very much and their inability to climax has nothing to do with the men they are with. She might be too tense for a variety of reasons. So, if at all possible, help her relax. Or, perhaps, she only needs to strengthen her vaginal muscles before she can feel certain sensations and achieve orgasm. The vagina is a muscular organ. The more you exercise it, the better it works. She can do the exercise described here.

The exercise is the same for men and women. You know the muscle you use to hold back urination? Well, it's the same muscle you exercise for pleasure enhancement. Contract—hold—release. Do this about fifteen to twenty times a day, or more if possible. A woman will be better able to squeeze and caress her man's penis with her vagina, while a man will slightly grow in diameter during intercourse. Your woman will be thrilled!

THE G-SPOT

To explore this area, have the woman you love lie down, knees bent and feet flat on the bed, with a small pillow under her buttocks. This brings all her feminine parts closer to your reach. The size and location of the G-Spot will vary from woman to woman, but it's usually about the size of a quarter, and lies two to three inches inside the vagina directly behind the pubic bone—which is to say toward the stomach and navel, and away from the buttocks.

Insert the length of your lubricated fingers into her vagina with the idea that twelve o'clock is pointing toward her navel. The G-Spot will be resting somewhere between eleven o'clock and one o'clock. It does not protrude, so you will have to do some patient exploring until you arouse it enough to feel it as it swells. Because it's surrounded with tissue and lies deep in the vaginal wall, it might be wise to apply a little more pressure than usual.

The G-Spot is the focal point of female sexual arousal. The kind of comments from the women who have experienced a G-Spot orgasm, are like this one from Nicole, a thirty-eight-year-old mother of two from Topeka: "I felt like I was swimming in a pool of water, the bed was soaked, I was soaked, and my husband was drowning. It was the hottest, most erotic sensation I have ever felt.

"If you've never had the experience, I suggest you do, because you can't possibly imagine how wild and uninhibited you become! Now I know where the expression 'wet the bed' comes from. The bed was definitely wet!"

Jane, forty-four, a talented television actress and divorced mother of two, joyfully confessed, "The entire eight years I was married, I was anal retentive and couldn't have a single orgasm without 'Dicky,' my vibrator. After my husband and I separated, I bought myself anatomy books, sex books, and X-rated videos. One night, I hid in the bathroom, urinated, and then explored. I read it was better to urinate first, because of the pressure against the bladder. With a finger, I felt the upper front wall of my vagina. I had trouble finding the G-Spot, so I applied firmer pressure. With my other hand, I pressed on the stomach area just above my pubic hairs. As I continued to massage, a small portion of tissue about the size of a quarter began to swell. My knees collapsed, my muscles contracted—I felt dizzy and weak. What an adventure!"

Several women concurred that the "doggy" position during intercourse is the most stimulating for a G-Spot orgasm, because a man's penis has better access to the anterior (front) wall of the vagina. For the G-Spot orgasm, most women will need firmer pressure to the anterior vagina, quick rhythm, and a lot of friction. However, there are always exceptions to the rule—others may need less pressure, slower rhythms, or not so much friction.

In the event you try everything possible to bring your woman to a G-Spot orgasm and are not successful, don't give up! You could buy a G-Spotter at the nearest sex-equipment store or order one from a catalogue. A G-Spotter is a vibrator curved at the top designed to reach her exact area. If in the beginning, you don't succeed, try, try, again. You're not a quitter!

Lenny, forty, a bricklayer, found his girlfriend Lorna's G-Spot by having her lie on her belly with her legs spread apart and her hips slightly elevated. He inserted his fingers, palm down, into her vagina, exploring the front wall—the one facing the bed. Lenny asked Lorna to move her pelvis in several ways to make contact with his fingers. She gave a pleasing sigh at one point, so he slowly increased the firmness of his touch. As he felt Lorna becoming more aroused, he slipped his other hand under her abdomen above her pubic hairs and slowly pressed. She was suddenly delirious with ecstasy as he picked her hips up and slowly inserted the head of his penis into her warm, wet vagina. He only gave her a couple of inches before Lorna was squirming and screaming, "Yes, yes, YESSSSSSSSSSSSS!" She was pulling, biting, talking dirty. Lorna said, "Lenny made my body talk in seven languages. Somebody needs to put my Lenny into mass production!"

Men have a spot, too—the prostate—which is the equivalent of the woman's G-Spot. Like women, men can have two types of orgasms: one brought on by the penis and one brought on by the prostate. The prostate is difficult for a man to find by himself, but a woman can locate it by gently exploring with her lubricated finger the area inside your rectum. If you lie on your back and *relax*, knees bent, feet on the bed, she can feel the soft mass which is a few inches inside the rectum on the anterior (front) rectal wall. You can also find the spot. Lie in the same position, insert your thumb or finger into your anus, and press it against the front wall of your rectum and massage downward toward the anus.

Orgasm—whether G-Spot or clitoral or vaginal or a mixture of all three—depends on the physiological and emotional makeup of the two lovers. The "perfect lovers" fit at all intersections, all conjunctions, and they must be nourished from all directions—chemistry, trust, relaxation, goodwill, and determination—to produce this unique, one-act extravaganza.

THE VENUS BUTTERFLY AND
OTHER SPECIALTIES

One technique is not going to work for every woman. It's not possible. So be ready to be adventurous, spontaneous, and inventive. If you want to be a great lover you should have the basic techniques of foreplay under your belt and a few specialties besides.

This does not mean voraciously rubbing your face, nose, and head in every part of her anatomy. I'm sure the girl would lie there motionless, waiting for that silly person to ejaculate and leave. To please a woman you must have a slow, firm hand and a knowing, tender touch, you must love what you're doing, who you're doing it with, and above all, you must have fun!

The Venus Butterfly is a highly erotic and stimulating way to give a woman a more satisfying orgasm. Even if it takes longer for her to climax, this method should promote a state of complete euphoria. And it should become effortless for you. It's about total body awareness—yours and hers. The delight of this motion is in the timing, the rhythm, and the right touch. Too hard can hurt, too soft is not effective. First, you need to understand it in your own mind before you try it on your woman.

Begin by assuming the missionary position, and penetrate her vagina with your penis. Feel her becoming more excited with your motion. Then—slow down! Now is the time to experience the Venus Butterfly. Grip her bent knees under both armpits, to give you control of her lower torso. Slide your cupped hands under her buttocks. In the proximity of her anal area let your hands arouse her by tapping your flat fingers firmly to the following rhythm: push in, tap once, pull out, tap twice. The timing is 1 and 1-2, 1 and 1-2. Tap, and tap, tap. Or vice versa: push in, tap twice, pull out, tap once. The timing is 1-2 and 1, 1-2 and 1. Tap, tap, and tap.

Another suggestion would be to thrust completely into her vagina while your fingers are fluttering like the wings of a butterfly in a firm, decisive rhythm—tap, tap, tap, tap, tap, tap, tap, tap, tap, tap. As fast as you can say it is how fast you should do it.

Some men will be more dextrous than others. It takes rhythm and practice. But, by making your woman feel you *know* exactly what you're doing, she will be able to open up completely to receive total satisfaction.

A number of women I interviewed were willing to experiment and later raved about the results. One sensuous girl named Carol commented, "I felt like it was the '*most woman*' I could ever be!" Darlene, a strong, sensitive teacher, said, "I felt he was completely in charge, so I surrendered!" Susan, a medical student in her mid-twenties, claimed, "My mind completely left me. I was totally hypnotized!"

There are other ways to enrich a woman's orgasm. Put both hands under her buttocks and at the final moment of her orgasm, squeeze both buttocks firmly in a quick rhythm that resembles the timing of the throb you experience when you ejaculate. At this moment, penetrate as deeply as you can. This will heighten her arousal and enhance her orgasm.

The stomach is a very sexy area. If you're behind her in a cuddle position, hold your thumb at the side of her waist while your forefingers simultaneously knead the area around the navel. If you're in front of her when you're having oral sex, penetrating, or when you're manually stimulating her, put the heels of both hands on her hip bones and knead her pelvis with your forefingers. This is a real pleasure zone for women.

Although the anus is rarely talked about, it can be a highly erotic area for both men and women. In men, touching or massaging the prostate can lead to ejaculation. Women can also experience highly erotic sensations from gentle stimulation in this area. But be careful, because the surrounding tissue is extremely sensitive. Some women prefer that you lick and gently suck it before you try to insert your finger because the anus is not self-lubricating. Brushing across the anus with your finger, or barely inserting your finger during intercourse can heighten her arousal. Also, during oral stimulation, you can insert your finger in her anus and work it rhythmically in time with or opposite your tongue in her vagina to bring on an incredible sensation.

I'm sure she will let you know immediately whether it pleases or displeases her. In the event she pushes your hand away, do you leave that area alone? This could this be an indication of too much delight that she feels uncomfortable experiencing, she may be embarrassed, or you may be stimulating improperly. Whatever the reason, if it's a turn-off to her, don't even pause—move on! You can ask her later what she didn't like about it.

There are many variations of oral sex. The best known is the classic sixty-nine position, in which both partners give one another oral stimulation. It can be done with both of you on your sides facing opposite ends or with one on top of the other facing opposite ends. If only the woman is receiving oral stimulation, usually she will lie on her back, her knees bent and her feet on the bed, while your head is between her legs. Certain women, such as Jenny, actually prefer to be sitting on your face, but you have to know how to keep her weight lightly over your face and gently control the situation by keeping the palms of your hands directly below the buttocks. A woman can usually orgasm more easily sitting on your mouth because she's able to control her rhythms to suit herself. Take care if she does prefer sitting on your face and has several orgasms, because she could see stars, get dizzy, and drop her entire body weight on your nose. When her thigh muscles start to vibrate, you know she has lost control! (Also see earlier section, Cunnilingus, in this chapter.)

There are a number of women who adore fellatio. Going down on their fellow is the next best thing to heaven. Many women have told me that it's highly erotic because they consider it taboo; it allows them to explore and free themselves from their inhibitions, especially when they swallow their man's semen at the end of the act. In a quote from *Playboy* magazine, comic Felecia Michaels said, "We like sex. We even like oral sex. What we don't like are the stupid questions you guys ask afterward. 'What does it taste like?' What are we supposed to say? 'Well, being a connoisseur of fine jizz, I would say that yours is full-bodied, dry, and unassuming.' "

What if oral sex makes you smile until your cheeks hurt, but your woman doesn't share your enthusiasm? First and foremost, don't grab her head and shove your apparatus into her mouth. She will never do it again (and may never see you again). The correct approach would be to tell her that you really enjoy it and often fantasize about her beautiful lips wrapped delicately around your magic wand. If she agrees to give it a go, make sure you're freshly scrubbed and smelling good. A whiff of anything unpleasant will be the final cut.

Spread a little of her favorite flavor over the military helmet. If your woman likes cherry flavor, try using that particular Rachel Perry Lip-Lover flavor. Maybe she prefers banana or any variety of flavors. Be patient, be gentle, smell good, and ask her to focus her lips, tongue, and energies on the frenulum, that half-inch wide band just south of the head. The spot is about three-quarters of an inch in diameter and it's at the inverted V of your helmet or hood. Whatever you do, don't even think about ejaculating in her mouth the first time. In fact, don't ejaculate until she becomes familiar with the process and learns to enjoy giving you pleasure. This may take some time.

Some lovers do manage to leave bruises on one another. Grace, who works out at my gym, has creamy white skin that bruises easily, and one day I called attention to the bruises on her legs. She told me that she and her guy lust for one another and get carried away in strange locations. She said it was unintentional and done in the sensual exploration of their love-making.

The possibilities truly are endless. Don't be afraid if something feels strange or uncomfortable the first few times you experiment. You may need to practice before there is any magic. This kind of magic rarely, if ever, happens overnight, except the sexual chemistry I spoke of earlier. By the same token, never shy away from letting your partner experiment with your body. Since she is going through the same experience and exploring her own senses, lie back and try to enjoy. It may accidentally hurt, tickle, or surprise you, but hold your own. This may be the only way she knows how to show you her deepest feelings of love and affection.

MASTURBATION FOR MEN

I started having sex when I was nine years old, but it wasn't until I was fourteen that I started doing it with girls.

—CHEVY CHASE

Never, never feel guilty about masturbating! Giving yourself a bit of titillation is a universal pastime, commonly practiced by all sexes and ages. It's wonderful for the complexion because it relieves tension, satisfies the sexual urge, and puts a smile on your face, even if it's momentary.

Every country has a myth about its repopulation after the mythical flood of eight or ten thousand years ago, when water filled the earth and few people survived. The sole survivor in India, for example, a demigod, was left sitting on a rock. His hand began to swell into a female sex organ. He placed that hand over his penis while gently massaging and stroking until he had an orgasm, and thereby created the first woman. A single act of masturbation created a whole generation of people. Even today, images of the hand as a female organ are etched in stone in the ruins of ancient Mexico and Peru.

In Persia and the Middle Eastern empires, the many wives of one man would undertake concubine training and vie to become the number-one wife by mastering the art of love. They learned by using their hands to explore their body sensations. Once they understood this pleasure, they would repeat the ritualistic experience on their master.

Only in learning to please yourself will you be able to please your partner. The act of fully giving pleasure to your own body is the art of masturbation. This ancient art is upheld even today by millions of men and women. It will aid you in learning your own sexual responses without putting undue pressure and demands on yourself and your partner. Once you've learned the key to turning on your own senses, you will be able to teach your woman how to give you optimum pleasure and a new world will open.

Students have told me that they masturbate to release anxieties and get more focused before taking exams. In my several interviews with high school and college students, I was told they masturbate together or separately in front of one another as a safe-sex practice for the 1990s. But lo and two beholds! Don't call a woman and say, "Hi, Mary Lou. You wanna come over to my house Friday night and jerk off?" That would be tactless. There's a nicer way of sliding into the moment. For instance, when you're on a date, as you're kissing and getting each other a little heated up, you might try whispering in her ear, "Do you enjoy touching yourself?" If she responds favorably, then you might say, "I think I would just explode if I could watch you touch yourself. It would stay with me for days." Or, while you're looking at each other and you feel her excitement rise, you could start touching yourself very gently, encouraging her to do the same to herself. During this communication, you should speak seductively and sensually while your eyes make love to her.

Don't be offended if a woman shies away from your suggestions. It doesn't mean she's frigid. It simply means she's unable to share the experience at that moment. There may be another time, another place, when she feels more adventurous.

Before I close this section, I must warn you against the pitfalls of masturbating too much. Now, what *is* too much—every day, several times a day? Yes, I think you're sliding into a danger zone. For whatever reason you developed the habit or addiction—and I've heard plenty of stories—*stop it!* You're only harming yourself. Just because you like chocolate candy are you going to eat a pound of chocolate every day? I don't think so.

For you to better understand the problems addiction can cause, here's Lew's story: "I started playing with myself when I was about five or six years old. Wearing Coke-bottle rim glasses, having buck teeth, and being skinny didn't help me win friends or influence enemies, especially girls. I was another sex-crazed adolescent attending an all-boys school who did what everybody else did to release—jerk off!

"I envied jocks who paraded beautiful women

around. I would've given my right testicle for just one of their leftovers. But instead, I masturbated my way through life, until I met my college sweetheart.

"I was a virgin, she wasn't. Everything went smoothly, until I started suffering from retarded ejaculation. I couldn't ejaculate and my erections lasted forever. Reassuring myself nothing was wrong, I broke up with her and started dating Pat. With Pat I could ejaculate, but not without erotic, visual stimulation.

"Pat suggested that I see a sex therapist. I did and learned that because I had become addicted to masturbation, I was disturbing my natural brain sensations and, subconsciously, preferred my hand to my woman; because I had learned to do it a certain way that no one could reproduce, I was hooked on self-pleasure. I had to make a decision, either stop jerkin' off or continue with my problem. Pat was patient. She worked with me through the difficulty. It took a few months, but I can honestly say that I prefer her mouth, her hands, and her pussy. Sure, I still do it sometimes, but I don't abuse the pleasure."

The cure for masturbation addiction is to get yourself into a regular relationship, communicate your problem, and make an effort toward having successful intercourse. Concentrate on satisfying the woman's needs, being in the moment, and forgetting yourself completely. Put all your focus on her pleasure. It really works!

MASTURBATION FOR WOMEN

"I discovered masturbation to orgasm when I was about 13, and I was sure nobody else had ever done it."

—ERICA JONG

Lysistrata, a Greek Classic play written by Aristophanes in 411 B.C., was an early attempt at womens' liberation through masturbation. Tired of the war against Sparta, and annoyed at their husbands' absence from bed, the Athenian women went on a sex strike. They refused to have sex with their men until the men agreed to stay home. I guess that would put an end to all wars!

At first, the men thought it was a bad joke, but each time they returned home, they were greeted with closed lips, legs, and arms. The women consoled themselves with eight-inch dildos. The men eventually broke down. Unable to tolerate celibacy, they made their peace.

In ancient Greece, dildos were made of leather or wood. Dildos of solid gold have been found in Miletus, intended for worship rather than personal use—oooh! too cold! That would be a chill and a thrill, although some dildos intended for use in the Orient were made of jade. Ivory was a warmer substance, and wax dildos may have been used but haven't survived. I'm sure women have always experimented with whatever materials were at hand.

Women have always done it—whether with candles, bananas, cucumbers, several fingers, or whatever they can find on the spot. (Some women cut the head of a cucumber into smooth ridges and warm it before insertion.) Obviously, nothing can compare to a man's penis, but a lot of women have difficulty finding the right man that can give them satisfaction, so they choose to do it themselves.

No two women masturbate the same way, just as no two women are alike in what turns them on. There's timing, rhythm, and self-expression to consider. During my research, Masters and Johnson and Shere Hite reported that 26 percent of masturbating women use vibrators, while 4 percent stimulate the clitoris by pulling back the hood. Almost 75 percent like masturbating on their backs, while 36 percent rub the clitoris with their fingers or other parts of the hand. Only 11 percent use more than one technique, and many women report playing with their nipples as part of the pleasure. Several women masturbate in front of a mirror or squatting over a mirror for added stimulation.

In a review of sexual dysfunction, Dr. Dickes and Dr. Lassen suggest that 46 percent of women almost never experience orgasm with male penetration alone. The good news is that most all the women I interviewed said they still prefer intercourse to masturbation. (Unfortunately for you guys, the lowest poll was fellatio!)

Certain women are unable to get enough sexual stimulation. They can orgasm five to six times a day, every day, and it's never enough. These females were usually born with a hormonal imbalance.

Most women use vibrators to stimulate the external parts. And a low of about 1.5 percent insert them into the vagina. However, women who feel guilty about using vibrators and gadgets will get stimulation by using pillows, blankets, or garments rolled up and rubbed against the clitoris. I feel that using a vibrator too often is dangerous for lovemaking. Too many quick fixes can make a woman slightly impatient with her man. Rarely can a man's fingers compete with a vibrator. It's healthier to alternate.

There are also women who cross and uncross their legs innumerable times to promote sexual arousal.

With their legs crossed, they squeeze their thighs tightly in rhythm until they bring on an orgasm.

Several athletic women I know are able to orgasm by doing a series of incline-board leg raises for their lower abdominals. They lie on an incline, hold on to the bar above their head, and with straight legs, raise them up high above the waist, hold for a few seconds and then lower them slowly down. They have to do at least three sets of twenty-five, maybe more, before the pain turns into a pleasurable orgasm. It doesn't happen to every girl and it doesn't happen every time.

Victoria, an auburn-haired, well-known television personality, suggested I mention the balls—Ben Wa balls, that is. Vicky likes to rock back and forth with them inserted into her vagina. Sometimes she even wears them on the set while she's working. They are basically electroplated steel ball bearings. Women in the Orient have enjoyed their pleasure for many years.

A woman inserts the balls (with an external string attached) into her vagina as she would a tampon. Since they are only three-quarters of an inch in diameter, she can walk around with them bouncing inside her while she has orgasm after orgasm. She can also enjoy intercourse, or any other kind of stimulation while the balls are inside. But coughing, laughing, or sneezing are out if you want to avoid sending the balls bouncing and rolling across the floor!

Victoria said she set off the metal detectors at the airport in New York during her book tour and caused pandemonium. She was terribly embarrassed!

The "Water Technique" is quite well known. It usually starts in childhood when girls discover that by lying in the tub, they can maneuver the genitals directly under the faucet's flow of water, controlling the stimulation until plateau turns into orgasm.

While in Paris during an interview with an effervescent woman named Monique, I learned about a more adult variation of the "Water Technique." While in school, Monique had earned a place on one of the prized athletic teams. Her coach was in the habit of using an unusual form of punishment for wayward behavior. Culprits were rushed to the showers, grabbed by the neck, and maneuvered in such a way that a harsh stream of water hit the groin, usually exciting orgasm and rendering a body limp. Monique said, "Most of the girls were unaware that having an orgasm was synonymous with 'shower' punishment. One minute we were in a rage and the next minute we were feeling good!"

If you see a woman crouched in the Jacuzzi just over the jet streams, you may want to leave her alone—or say, "Excuse me, ma'am, I think I could do it better!"

Does masturbating destroy a woman's sexual desire for her man? Women can also feel anxiety toward sex, just as you might. Her sex drive may be higher than yours, so she orgasms before a date. Or, if you're not feeding or fulfilling her adventurous side, she may masturbate to the point of arousal. Masturbating doesn't mean coming, although that's generally the goal. If she's compelled to stimulate herself before, during, and after sex with you, then masturbation is not the problem. It may be her anxiety toward sex, or you. In which case, you need to have a talk. I'm sure you will find the remedy. Masturbation is by no means harmful; it can be extremely helpful. You are "loving" yourself!

THE JOY OF CONDOMS

No glove, no love.

The facts of life in the 1990s are clear: Condoms are here to stay.

It's plain and simple: Now is not the time to be like Evel Knievel and flirt with death. You are just beginning to discover the lover in you, and you want to be around for a long time to enjoy your new-found skills! Which means that to our sense of adventure we need to add *responsibility*. Responsibility should be for your own health (with exercise, rest, and the proper nutrients to keep your immune system in peak condition) and for your relations with others. If promiscuity is on your mind, then please keep it there (or at least, under your hat!).

Like the Boy Scouts of America, you should always "be prepared"—in all areas of life. Nowhere is it more important than in lovemaking. Not only do condoms reduce the risk of unwanted pregnancy but also the rapid spread of STDs (sexually transmitted diseases), especially HIV. If you want to have a long and happy love life free from the fear of diseases and unplanned children, then you must include condoms in your love repertoire.

The condom goes by many names—rubber, prophylactic, skin, jimmie hat, Frenchie, and raincoat—but whatever you call it, it should definitely be carried with you at all times. Do not store it in very hot places or in freezing temperatures, or where it could get crunched or punctured (like in your wallet). Increasing numbers of women are now carrying condoms with them, as studies have shown that women have a greater risk than men of contracting HIV from heterosexual intercourse.

Condoms are easily purchased in most drugstores,

grocery stores, and in many variety and specialty shops. They come in various shapes, styles, and colors, though there are basically two types of material used: lambskin and latex. Neither health officials nor I recommend the lambskin variety, as it is a porous membrane and will not stop transmission of HIV and other diseases. (Men who get irritated by latex, however, can roll on a lambskin first, then put the latex condom over it.)

Some variety stores carry a rainbow of colors and novelty condoms, such as Glow Worms, French Ticklers, Studs, Flavors, and other such variations. Some of these have moveable rubberized tips having the appearance of a balloon not fully inflated. Others have ridges designed to give women a heightened sensation of a penis. There are those that glow in the dark (but could be carcinogenic), and those that have some flavor, like mint (although most women prefer real fruit). And finally the "super large" variety that are designed to titillate the imagination of both partners. Choose your fantasy! (Make sure you read the label's fine print.)

We can't talk about condoms without also talking about lubrication. It's *very important* that you use a good lubricant for several reasons. First, you don't want to hurt the woman. If she's not fully wet when you begin, you may make her feel uncomfortable. And second, if you do manage to cause an abrasion of her skin, that is one more possible pathway for a virus to travel. Some condoms come prelubricated, but it's best if you buy your own. Be sure to use *water-based* lubricants only that also contain the spermicide Nonoxyl-9. Oil-based wetting agents, such as baby oil, mineral oil, body lotions, vegetable oil, or petroleum jelly, will cause the latex in the condom to disintegrate! There are numerous water-based products on the market such as KY Jelly, Astroglide, and Wet. Just ask your pharmacist or doctor if you need advice.

If you're not familiar with condoms, it's possible to put one on the wrong way, rendering it—and you—ineffective. Test it first by unrolling the rolled-up part a little to be sure you're putting it on the right way. Then grasp the very tip between your thumb and forefinger to create a pocket for the ejaculate to collect, and roll the condom down your shaft, all the way to the base. If you don't feel comfortable yet with using a condom, then buy a few inexpensive types to practice with. The last thing you want after a hot session of foreplay, where your lady is overcome with your smoldering passion and begging you to take her to the limit, is to fumble around trying to figure out how to put on your jimmie hat! Have a sense of perspective.

Now, I'm sure you're thinking at this point, How do I talk about condoms? I know you think they're a pretty clinical subject, and to some of you they may even seem like the kiss of death to romance. And granted, there are a few women out there who simply will not talk about them, like Sonya, thirty-six, a film editor: "I refuse to talk about condoms with my men. They either put them on swiftly and quietly at the right moment, or they're history."

But Sonya is definitely an exception. To most of today's women, "condom consciousness" is the sign of an intelligent mind. And intelligence is sexy, remember? When the time is right, just bring up the subject directly and with confidence. Watch your woman's eyes when you talk this talk, and you will be able to gauge her feelings more clearly. You might add that you are free from all diseases (assuming you are, of course), and that you passed your most recent blood test (if you have). If you have been celibate or are with only one woman for a length of time, she would want to know that as well. Be honest and straightforward—and the woman will respect you for being so considerate of yourself and her.

Of the many women I interviewed for this book, about half said that they disliked the idea of condoms, and the other half said they could enjoy sex more knowing that they were protected. However, most of the women demanded them *without fail!* So, men, condoms are here to stay. They are an integral part of loving in the 1990s, so you might as well make friends with them now!

I asked Terry, a freshman at the University of Texas, if she used condoms. She replied, "Are you kidding? I wouldn't let a man touch me without a condom. My motto is 'No balloon, no party!' " If you know that your partner is actively dating more than one person, then you *must* wear a condom—never knowingly go unprotected.

My friend of many years, Amy, told me, "I always stop at a certain point to ask the man if he has protection. If he starts putting on his sunglasses, he obviously doesn't have a clue. Then it's time for my tray of assorted condoms! But if he produces one, I know the brother's clean!"

I'm sure many of you men have a strong prejudice against condoms for the following reasons: You feel that in order for the lady to appreciate your "little gentleman" (or large gent, as the case may be) she needs to be exposed to it directly, or that it doesn't feel the same to you when you wear one. Those are false and dangerous assumptions. If she adores the "little guy," there's plenty of get-acquainted games she can play prior to intercourse.

Eloise, an LSU undergraduate, tells of her boyfriend, Lewis, who would instantly lose his erection when trying to put on a condom. "Lewis hates condoms! He feels he's losing his manliness by covering it up. I disagree. What if he gets an itch and I'm not around to scratch it? If I can get him in the habit of using one, I'll feel a lot more comfortable and protected."

Some women are even making trips to specialty shops to learn more about condoms. Gayle, a nineteen-year-old ballet student in my class, confided that she has made several trips to local shops, asked for printed information on their use, and purchased several different makes to familiarize herself with them. She's also learning about the new woman's condom made of polyurethane that's been approved by the FDA. It's supposed to be 40 percent stronger than latex—check it out!

If you're afraid that condoms may "spoil the moment" in your lovemaking, then think again. Women in the nineties have accepted them as a necessary part of sex, and with a little creativity on your part, you can make them "sexy" as well. As a well-known gynecologist in Beverly Hills told me, "It's all a matter of attitude and breaking down previous conditioning." First of all, be conscious of your timing. Wait for the perfect moment; rushing may find you reaching for Mr. Raincoat just as her mouth is reaching for Mr. Big. Bad timing! Be patient. If she offers you a selection of condoms on a tray, choose one quickly and get on with it, or ask her if she has a preference.

The act of putting on a condom can be just as sexy as using it. Take your time—romance the act, as well as your woman. You may want to massage your lady with it at first, sliding it gently along her inner thighs, over her vaginal lips, over her clitoris (with two fingers in the condom). She may want to taste it first. (Be sure there is no lubricant on it beforehand.) And allow her the pleasure of putting it on your swollen member—that can be very erotic for us! All in all, try to make this procedure fit in with the rest of your fantasies.

Martin, forty-four, a social worker in Atlanta, said, "I feel like a clown with that rubber thing on. You know, silly." Herman, twenty-nine, a policeman in New Jersey, said, "I'm fairly large, so when I put the cap on down below, I look like a rubber 'hot dog.' My girlfriend makes it part of foreplay. She opens it and licks all around, while rolling it down. At first, it felt like that old joke about licking an ice cream cone through a window pane. But now we're used to it and it feels pretty good!"

Once you've released your love juices, be sure to withdraw your penis *before* it begins to soften. Make certain to hold onto the base of the condom so you won't leave it inside your woman and so no semen will leak from the base. Once you've safely withdrawn so there is no chance for spillage of semen, you can begin to lavish your woman with all the affection she deserves.

Well, that's the condom story. Let me close with another story. Jack and Jerry were walking down a forest path, when suddenly they saw a big black bear running after them. They ran as fast as they could, and climbed up a tree. The bear began to climb the tree after them. Jack pulled out a pair of track shoes and quickly put them on. Jerry asked, "What are you doing?" Jack replied, "When the bear gets close enough, we'll drop out of the tree and start running." Jerry said, "You fool—don't you know you can't out-run a bear?" Jack countered, "I don't have to outrun the bear—I just have to outrun *you!*"

The moral of this story is obvious, as is the moral to the condom story. Be like Jack—be smart, be prepared, think ahead—and you'll be around a lot longer to enjoy your lovemaking skills.

5

....

If Things
Go Wrong:
Troubleshooting

The only abnormality is the incapacity to love.
—ANAÏS NIN

PREMATURE EJACULATION

Is that a gun in your pocket, or are you just happy to see me?

—MAE WEST

When should an ejaculation be called "premature"? Most men reach orgasm within two minutes of starting coitus. Normal is anything from ten seconds to three minutes. Yet today, men think they are coming too quickly when they last five minutes. Time is irrelevant: They come too soon only if the woman doesn't have her orgasm first or simultaneously. (There are no statistics regarding how long an erection can or should last.)

Don't be like a bull that loses it all with one second-long thrust or like an elephant who spends thirty seconds impregnating his mate! That's not very encouraging for a woman. But rather be like a sleek greyhound, who makes entry and thrusts away for twenty to thirty seconds, then swirls his leg over her and turns around 180 degrees. They stay locked together but facing in opposite directions for up to thirty minutes. Not bad for a canine!

Certain men will try all kinds of things to last longer, such as numbing the penis with a topical anesthetic. But premature ejaculation is not caused by an overly sensitive penis; it's simply lack of emotional control. You can learn how to control your orgasm.

Start by taking your penis in your hand and stimulating yourself until you almost reach orgasm. Stop for a few seconds, long enough for your excitement to simmer down a bit. Then stroke the shaft and tip once again, until you almost climax. Repeat this three or four times. Each time stop just before you peak. If you feel you're going to lose control and ejaculate, immediately squeeze the base of your penis with your thumb and index finger and hold it until the sensation passes. Better yet, grab your testicles and pull them down. At the fourth or fifth peak, ejaculate.

By far the best solution is to bring the woman to orgasm with your tongue or by touching and stroking her *before* you penetrate. This way, if you're premature, nothing is lost! Take your sweet time and practice with her.

Arousal is a wonderful state of euphoria. When you feel yourself getting ready to explode before the woman is ready, hold back, and make the pause a part of foreplay as if teasing her before you go on. This pause will allow you to cool down and extend the act a little longer, until the woman is begging you to finish it. You can then reenter triumphantly.

If you're embarking on a date with a new woman and the thought of her fires up your "sex pistol" while you're getting dressed, stop and take a few minutes to masturbate. Then go to fetch her. If you have the time, and you know this problem is constant, do it three or four hours earlier. If you're a sexually overstimulated man, doing it a few minutes before could trigger a desire for immediate penetration—and that's exactly what you're trying to avoid!

Maury, a young doctor, uses masturbation as an aid to sustain from ejaculating too soon. His preference is doing it immediately before walking out the door. It doesn't affect his style; he still desires the woman just as much, if not more, but it allows him to be more controlled while on a date and making love.

Take care, because a man should be able to maintain his cool throughout an evening with a beautiful, sexy woman without her suspecting she's been the subject of his erotic fantasies. If you look like a fire-eating dragon every time she crosses her legs or sighs, that's definitely not cool. To get another date with this beauty, you must appear as if you're in control and confident. Then the odds of getting what you ultimately want will be in your favor.

George, a musician, says he takes more time on foreplay and gives a woman as much pleasure as possible, because he has an ejaculation problem. His method is to stop and pull out. George deemphasizes the "main event" by diverting his thoughts from lovemaking to other things like the sun, the moon, a cold shower, changing the oil in his motorcycle, or whatever springs to mind for a few minutes. Then he reenters and all is well.

Bobby, a stockbroker, sheds his prematurity problem by hitting his toe on something, pinching himself, biting the pillow, or knocking his fist against the bedpost. He conjures up any manner of distractions. He says they're always different and they always work.

Seth, a writer, has a statistical kind of brain, and he gets busy thinking of stats. "Avoid the doggy position at all costs, it's instant come!"

Phil, a movie director, said, "I go very slowly. It's the secret for me. Because the minute I start to pump in a faster rhythm, I become too excited and it's all over. After much ado, I've finally found a trick that works. Taking a great deal of time with my woman, pleasing her, releases the pressure from me.

"Orgasm is a throbbing feeling you get when you come," Phil added, "but you don't necessarily have to come to have that feeling. What I do is take it to the limit by letting my penis throb a few times. It's actually an orgasm of testicular contractions—a trigger, so to speak. It feels like I'm coming, but I'm not. It takes a lot of practice because the muscles in my legs and pelvis are filled with tension. I relax and let the tension go. A while later, the muscles go into spasms, and the semen is squeezed out . . . ejaculation!''

Jed, a great lover of women, said, "Don't tell anybody my secret, but I use alternate speeds. When I think I am losing it, I slow down to one-third the speed I was at originally and think of something I like about the woman—her beauty, her personality. It's funny; I'm an athlete, but I never think of sports. You've got to live in the moment to be a good lover."

OK, there may be times when you can't come at all. Just remember that your mind is your most erogenous zone. If the problems are, for example, that you are infatuated with the woman, you had a bad day at work, too much stress, or a death in the family, you cannot direct your body to pleasure. The key is to *relax*, even at the risk of losing the erection.

Mentally step away—think about your total being. Change your focus from sex to something that gives you peace and pleasure: fishing, swimming, the rain, a waterfall, diving into a cold lake, the beach in winter. After you've done this, look at your woman with renewed interest and you will feel a special warmth. And guess what? You'll orgasm.

Also, be aware that your urinary tract and sexual organs are the same. If either one is being used, the other is affected. So if you have a full bladder, it could prevent you from ejaculating. The pressure will take over and you won't be able to ejaculate. Remember to take care of this beforehand. You see, the real secret is to talk to your private area with your mind. Tell *it* what to do. Don't let it tell *you* what to do. Use your mind!

Thinking about other things during lovemaking may be an effective way to postpone ejaculation, but it's no way to achieve harmony with your partner, who will probably resent your absentmindedness. However, there is a pleasure enhancer called "Long Joy," developed in China, based on an ancient herbal formula, and available for purchase in the United States. It will increase a man's endurance for an extended period. How long? That's up to you and your skills of mind control!

WHEN YOU CAN'T GET IT UP OR KEEP IT UP

At some point in a man's life, he will suffer from temporary impotence. This occurs in about 10 percent of the adult male population. Some older men suffer from recurring impotence, which can be treated either with an injection of the drug papaverine or with an apparatus such as a penile splint or implant, or even an artificial penis. But for most men, this saying is true: "If you don't use it you might lose it!" After all, there's muscle at the base of the penis and muscles need exercise. You certainly don't want to fall into an asexual mode from a lengthy abstinence.

Men who have active sex lives are the lucky ones, because they are more likely to avoid the curse of impotence during old age. In a Kinsey report, a seventy-one-year-old man still enjoyed seven orgasms a week, and an eighty-eight-year-old man was said to be extremely sexually active with his ninety-year-old wife!

Impotence is usually self-induced by a negative mental attitude. Some men feel inferior or inadequate because they lack length or width. Some have been in accidents that left them altered or scarred and feel they can't satisfy women or that they will think they're unattractive. This negative attitude is downright silly and deprives men of fun and pleasure. A few visits to a specialty clinic or, better still, a tender, loving woman usually cures this malady.

Ask yourself what the problem is. It may be one of these common explanations: the wrong woman, anxiety about your performance, fear of intimacy, depression or stress, guilt due to religion or self-imposed ethics, or the influence of alcohol and drugs.

THE WRONG WOMAN

Your mind is the most erogenous part of your body, and when the mind is turned off, your penis follows. Maybe you were overcome with lust for her body, but once you got to bed, she babbled incessantly or her personal hygiene turned you off. Or maybe she criticized you until you were overcome with self-doubt. Self-doubt is bad for your erection. You need a relaxed, confident state of mind to have an erection.

It could also be that the woman you are with is not fulfilling your deepest desires. Maybe you need more mental stimulation, or simply more fun in the relationship. If this is the case, you need to examine yourself and your relationship thoroughly and work out a solution.

ANXIETY ABOUT YOUR PERFORMANCE

Performance anxiety in sex creates serious problems for the male. You see a beautiful woman, and a whiff of her perfume ignites your flame; in your fantasies everything is magical. But when you get her in bed, nothing works! Why? You were probably *so* intimidated by her beauty, charm, intellect, or whatever else held you captive that you tried to give a performance instead of being yourself and enjoying her. Instead of loving her, you were outside yourself observing and, perhaps, criticizing what you were doing—and maybe what she was doing as well. Obviously, you'll always find faults and shortcomings if you look hard enough.

But what's the point, if it means you will lose your goal of giving pleasure to her and yourself?

FEAR OF INTIMACY

My girlfriend, Susie, tells this story: "The first week after I moved in with my boyfriend Phil, sex was dynamic. Shortly thereafter, he had trouble getting an erection. I, of course, blamed myself, but he reassured me I was not the problem. We talked for hours on end to find a solution.

"Finally, a door opened when he confessed that his mother was a domineering and doting woman and that he feared I would be the same. When we were intimate, he became afraid of the closeness and lost his erection. Knowing this information, I did my best to convince him that I wasn't like his mother and had no intentions of controlling his life.

"I suggested that we take separate bedrooms until we became better acquainted. I gave him a lot of space, and patiently waited. In less than two months I gained his trust. Late one night, during a thunderstorm, he crawled into my bed and, like a man who had been in prison for twenty years, he devoured every inch of my body. Lucky me!"

DEPRESSION AND STRESS

Depression and stress are the most common dampeners of a man's sexual appetite. When a man is depressed, there's little he cares for, especially sex. Going through any kind of transition—losing your job or someone special—can create tensions and zap a lot of your energy.

Please don't worry about your sexual appetite diminishing at certain times in your life. You're not an automaton; you're a human being, so relax and stop worrying. It happens to every man at some time or another. Just be patient; there is really nothing wrong with you. A change in your sleeping or eating patterns is sufficient to explain the change in your sex drive. All unpleasant things have a way of passing. It's the pleasant things that stay, and good sex can be one of the most pleasant things in your life!

DRUGS AND ALCOHOL

In our society, drug use has exploded to alarming proportions. Drugs create a lifeless, barren world of illusion. There's no room for health, nature, work, family, love, and least of all, sex. When a person gets high he loses perspective. He might think he's giving and getting great sensations, while the woman sees him as a poor soul who's not participating or interacting with her life.

An amazing number of women told me they had ended affairs because the man didn't satisfy them emotionally or sexually due to his abuse of drugs or alcohol. If you drown out sex with intoxicants, you're missing out on the greatest of all highs. Don't kid yourself: you're embarking on the path to self-destruction and should seek the help of caring friends or a competent counselor. And don't ever, ever wonder why all the women that were in your life have left you.

Epilogue

All right fellas, now that you've been given the keys to a woman's world of seduction, it's up to you to start using them. Many men throughout the ages have succeeded in walking through that golden door: Casanova, Beau Brummel, Don Juan, Rudolph Valentino, Clark Gable, to name just a few. *You* have their potential. You have the ability and I've given you the tools. As you learn to use them on a daily basis, confidence will develop naturally. Action with conviction is the bottom line.

Express yourself like a gentleman and your better qualities will surface, making you not only a consummate lover but a dynamic human being. And romance is the result of sharing these qualities with a woman.

You can *be anything* and *do anything*, if only you desire and persevere enough! Nothing can hold you back but your own fear. Know exactly what you want, work for it with all of your energy and enthusiasm, and become the exciting and irresistible person you were meant to be!

Sex Quiz

Now that you've read the book, how do you honestly rate yourself as a lover, both in and out of bed? You may want to read it again and even carry it around with you—just in case.

— Do you clean up and dress up for your date?
— Are you spontaneous, adventuresome, and *romantic?*
— Do you make false promises or verbally manipulate as a method of seduction?
— While on a date, do you flirt with the waitress, eye every attractive woman in the room, and comment on their physical attributes?
— Do you, without receiving affirmative, encouraging signals, put your hands all over your date?
— Are you inclined to "act the gentleman" only in the beginning of a relationship, then take her for granted?
— Do you know the kind of etiquette women love at dinner? At home? Do you know what things turn a woman off?
— Do you masturbate so often that during penetration you have difficulty staying erect without visual stimulation?
— Do you spend enough time on foreplay that you have her begging for more?
— Do you use condoms? Are you skilled in making them part of sex?
— Do you tease during intercourse to drive a woman dizzy with delight?

— Are you skilled at cunnilingus?
— Can you successfully find a woman's G-Spot?
— Do you know how to give a woman multiple orgasms?
— Do you know what women want after lovemaking?

With experience and application you will answer all these questions correctly, make their content second nature, and eventually develop a style that is all your own—exciting, unique, a true measure of manhood. Bon voyage!

Bibliography

ABLEMAN, PAUL. *The Sensuous Mouth*. New York: Ace, 1969.

ARCHER, W. G., ed. *The Kama Sutra of Vatsyayana*. New York: G. P. Putnam's Sons, 1963.

BARR, TONY. *Acting for the Camera*. Boston: Allyn and Bacon, Inc., 1982.

COWAN, CONNELL, AND KINDER, MELVYN. *Smart Women, Foolish Choices*. New York: Clarkson N. Potter, 1985.

ELISOFON, ELIOT, AND WATTS, ALAN. *Erotic Spirituality*. New York: The Macmillan Co., 1971.

FENSTERHEIM, HERBERT, AND BAER, JEAN. *Don't Say Yes When You Want to Say No*. New York: Dell Publishing Co., 1975.

GAWAIN, SHAKTI. *Creative Visualization*. Mill Valley, Calif.: Whatever Publishing, Inc., 1978.

GREENE, GAEL. *Delicious Sex*. New York: Prentice Hall Press, 1986.

KEEN, SAM. *Fire in the Belly*. New York: Bantam Books, 1991.

KENDALL, HENRY O., KENDALL, FLORENCE P., AND WADSWORTH, GLADYS E. *Muscles: Testing and Function.* 2d ed. Baltimore: The Williams and Wilkins Co., 1971.

LADAS, ALICE K., WHIPPLE, BEVERLY, AND PERRY, JOHN D. *The G-Spot.* New York: Holt, Rinehart, and Winston, 1982.

LAWRENCE, D. H. *Lady Chatterley's Lover.* New York: Signet, 1959.

LLOYD, JOAN E. *Nice Couples Do.* New York: Warner Books, Inc., 1991.

LORING, JOHN. *Tiffany Parties.* New York: Doubleday, 1989.

M. *The Sensuous Man.* New York: Dell Publishing Co., 1971.

MILONAS, ROLF. *Fantasex.* New York: Grosset & Dunlap Publishers, 1975.

MORGENSTERN, MICHAEL. *How to Make Love to a Woman.* New York: Ballantine Books, 1982.

NIN, ANAÏS. *Aphrodisiac.* New York: Crown Publishers, 1976.

PARSONS, ALEXANDRA. *Facts & Phalluses.* New York: St. Martin's Press, 1989.

PENNEY, ALEXANDRA. *How to Make Love to a Man.* New York: Clarkson N. Potter, 1981.

POST, ELIZABETH L. *Emily Post's Etiquette*. 14th ed. New York: Harper & Row Publishers, 1984.

REICH, WILHELM. *The Function of the Orgasm*. New York: Simon & Schuster, 1973.

REINISCH, JUNE M. *The Kinsey Institute New Report on Sex*. New York: St. Martin's Press, 1990.

SCHWARZENEGGER, ARNOLD. *Encyclopedia of Modern Body Building*. New York: Simon & Schuster, 1985.

RUTGERS, J. *How to Attain and Practice the Ideal Sex Life*. New York: Cadillac Publishing Co., 1940.

SHEPARD, MARTIN. *Ecstasy*. New York: Moneysworth, 1977.